D0897563

# SO SUE ME!

*Previous Books by James Yaffe*

NOVELS

*The Good-for-Nothing*
*What's the Big Hurry?*
*Nothing but the Night*
*Mister Margolies*
*Nobody Does You Any Favors*
*The Voyage of the Franz Joseph*

NONFICTION

*The American Jews*
Portrait of a Split Personality

SHORT-STORY COLLECTION

*Poor Cousin Evelyn and Other Stories*

# SO
# SUE ME!

*The Story of a Community Court*

JAMES YAFFE

*Saturday Review Press*

NEW YORK

*Copyright © 1972 by James Yaffe*

All rights reserved. No part of this work may be reproduced or transmitted in any form or by any means, electronic or mechanical, including photocopy, recording, or any information storage and retrieval system, without permission in writing from the publisher.

*Published simultaneously in Canada by*
*Doubleday Canada Ltd., Toronto.*

*Library of Congress Catalog Card Number: 72–79045*

*ISBN 0-8415-0210-2*

*Saturday Review Press*
*230 Park Avenue*
*New York, New York 10017*

PRINTED IN THE UNITED STATES OF AMERICA

*Design by Tere LoPrete*

*To the memory of my parents, Florence Scheinman Yaffe and Samuel Yaffe, this book is fondly dedicated. I hope they would have enjoyed it.*

# *Acknowledgment*

The friendly cooperation of the Jewish Conciliation Board has been indispensable to me in the writing of this book. I have been allowed free access to their files, with no strings attached, no attempt at censoring or influencing my opinions. I wish to thank everyone connected with the organization, but especially Mrs. Ruth Richman, its executive director, surely one of the hardest-working, most compassionate, and least appreciated people in the world of American Jewish social work.

My thanks also to Dr. Israel Goldstein, past president of the board, who graciously spoke to me at length about the board's history, purposes, and achievements, and the part he played in them.

The Jewish Room of the New York Public Library, with its splendid microfilm collection of Yiddish newspapers going back to the turn of the century, was invaluable to me. Every scholar (or semi-scholar, like myself) who is interested in any aspect of American Jewish life has reason to be grateful for the existence of this extraordinary facility.

Finally, my special thanks to Mrs. Sonia Hagalili, who assisted me in some of the most difficult aspects of my research. I will always be grateful to her for her intelligence, her energy, and her good humor. And my children loved her cookies.

# Contents

|   | Prelude | 3 |
|---|---------|---|
| 1 | Purpose | 7 |
| 2 | Procedure | 15 |
| 3 | Conciliation | 32 |
| 4 | Decision | 40 |
| 5 | Prestige | 53 |
| 6 | Lovers | 64 |
| 7 | Husbands and Wives—One | 84 |
| 8 | Husbands and Wives—Two | 98 |
| 9 | Husbands and Wives—Three | 121 |
| 10 | Parents | 136 |
| 11 | Children | 152 |
| 12 | Brothers and Sisters | 180 |
| 13 | Friends and Acquaintances | 194 |
| 14 | Worshipers | 219 |

# Contents

15  *Old People*                                    *245*
16  *Hopes*                                         *264*
    *Postlude*                                      *270*
    *Note:* On the Research in This Book            272

# SO SUE ME!

# *Prelude*

We are in a courtroom. There are three judges sitting side by side. There are spectators, reporters, stenographers. The next case is called—"Max Warshaw versus the Yehupetz Benevolent Society."

Warshaw, a man in his fifties, is the plaintiff. Quietly but angrily he explains his charges to the judges. "This society was founded over fifty years ago by a group of immigrants, *landsmen*, who came to America from the same village in Russia. Each member paid yearly dues, and from these dues benefits were paid when a member got sick, and when he dies, an endowment was to be given to his widow or his children to help them cover the funeral expenses. My father belonged to this *landsmanshaft* from the beginning. Last month he passed away. Now the society refuses to give me the endowment, which comes to three hundred dollars, though I am his only child and heir."

"What reason do they have for their refusal?" asks one of the judges.

"They claim my father signed a paper two years ago waiving his benefits for the privilege of paying no more dues. I am not a rich man, but I am not poor either. If I don't get the three hundred dollars, I will not go under. But I think there is a principle involved here."

"How old was your father when he died, Mr. Warshaw?"

"He was eighty-five years old."

The judges now ask to hear the other side of the story. Several officers of the society are present in court, huddling together, conferring with one another in low voices. Their official spokesman is the president of the society, Sanford Schloss. He is also in his fifties.

He opens his defense by showing the judges the paper that the late Reuben Warshaw signed. The judges look it over carefully. They ask Max Warshaw if he recognizes his father's signature, and he admits that he does.

"Mr. Schloss," says one of the judges to the president, "how long did Reuben Warshaw pay dues to your society?"

"We can't tell exactly," Schloss answers.

"You can tell it was a long time though, can't you? Since Reuben Warshaw was eighty-five years old when he died. And how much do your dues come to every year?"

"Ten dollars per year."

"Then tell me, Mr. Schloss, what did Mr. Warshaw gain by signing this document? Why should a man who is eighty-three years old forfeit all his payments for fifty years, with the knowledge that he doesn't have many more years to go?"

Schloss gives a shrug. "That is not our business. After all, nobody knows how long he will live."

Another judge speaks up. "Sensibly, though, do you think that a man eighty-three years of age would sign away a three hundred dollar endowment to save himself ten dollars a year? In order to break even, he would have to live to be one hundred and thirteen."

"*I* don't know what this man was thinking," says Schloss. "I only know that he approached me over and over again, requesting that I relieve him of his dues, and we always put him off. But two years ago, when he approached me again, I told him I would bring it up to the other officers, and it was agreed among us that Brother Warshaw be relieved of his dues for the remainder of his life. Afterwards we always asked him if he was satisfied, and he always said he was."

The judges turn to Max Warshaw. "Was your father senile in his last years? Not in his right mind? Did he perhaps not realize what he was signing?"

"I'm sorry, gentlemen, he wasn't senile. His mind was very alert."

"Then why do you think he signed this document?"

"I think it might have been because he had no money of his own, and I took care of all his needs. Maybe he thought he was doing me a favor by saving me the expense of these dues. All his life he was very independent—it wasn't easy for him to take money from his son."

The judges turn sternly back to Schloss. "I must say," says one of them, "that this makes a terrible impression on me. How can a society of decent people do such a thing, to take away his rights from a poor old man?"

"I concur," says another judge. "This strikes me as highly indecent."

"You will all step out of the court," says the third judge, "while we consider our decision."

We will stop the scene here to ask a few questions. What sort of muddleheaded judges are these? A document vital to the case is given to them, and they don't even bother to mark it and introduce it officially as evidence. Nobody remembers to swear in any of the witnesses, to put them on oath to tell the truth. Where are the lawyers for each side, prepared to cross-examine the opposing side? What right do the judges have to call the defendant names and refer to him as indecent before they have even begun to discuss the evidence? Worst of all, what about the judge's question to the plaintiff about his father's senility and whether or not the old man was in his right mind? Surely it is most unethical for a judge to suggest a line of argument to one of the parties in a case. On that point alone wouldn't any court of appeals reverse the decision if it happened to be in favor of the plaintiff?

But the strangest thing is that nobody seems to be bothered by any of these irregularities. No buzz of disapproval from the spectators, no objections from the defendants. Least perturbed of all are the judges themselves.

What kind of a court is this anyway?

# CHAPTER

# 1

## *Purpose*

The Jewish Conciliation Board was founded in 1920 by
Louis Richman, a lawyer, and Samuel Buckler, a rabbi.
This combination was significant. From the beginning
the Board represented a union between the complex
principles of American law and the rather different but
equally complex principles of the Jewish rabbinical tradition. Throughout its history the organization has been
kept alive by rabbis and lawyers working together.

Even in 1920 the idea behind the Board was neither
new nor revolutionary. It was one of the oldest ideas in
Jewish communal life. The Beth Din—the rabbinical
court—has probably existed in one form or another for
thousands of years. It was to a kind of Beth Din that the
elders brought their accusations against Susannah;
Daniel, rendering judgment with a mixture of piety
and worldly wisdom, was behaving not much differently from the judges of the Jewish Conciliation Board

today. After biblical times rabbinical courts continued to flourish throughout Europe, usually with the sanction of the Christian authorities. We have records of some that go back to the early Middle Ages. Until the advent of the Nazis every small self-contained Jewish community, every *shtetl* and ghetto, could be expected to have its own Beth Din.

In Israel the Beth Din has become a part of the official court system. Certain matters—divorce, for instance—fall within the sole jurisdiction of rabbinical courts, and in other matters the Israeli citizen is given a choice; an Israeli wife, when she sues her husband for support, may bring the case to either a civil or a rabbinical court.

In 1920, when Louis Richman got the idea for what was to become the Jewish Conciliation Board, he was in his twenties and just starting a career as a lawyer. He had been born in Latvia and brought to New York's Lower East Side as a small boy. His father was a dealer in religious articles and had business and social relations with many rabbis and talmudic scholars. Young Richman grew up listening to these men discussing, analyzing, disputing, and he developed a respect for their kind of half-spiritual, half-legalistic approach to the problems of human justice. Later, as a novice lawyer, he saw many cases in civil court that had specifically Jewish, often religious overtones. Once he saw an Irish judge deliver an unjust decision in a case having Jewish ramifications he was totally unable to understand. The judge's fury at the strange, garbled, "foreign" notions he was being forced to consider convinced Richman of the need for a court where Jewish people could get "Jewish justice." He enlisted the aid of Rabbi Buckler, and they set about adapting the old idea of the Beth Din to the new American climate.

The organization got off to a shaky start. The co-founders soon had their differences and split apart. For a while Rabbi Buckler set up a competing court. But he was driven back to the pulpit when Richman succeeded in getting Dr. Israel Goldstein interested in the project. Dr. Goldstein was a prominent "uptown" rabbi, an indefatigable officeholder in a multitude of important Jewish organizations, with connections among wealthy and distinguished Jewish laymen. (Though he retired from the rabbinate and went to live in Israel ten years ago, he still exerts considerable influence in American Jewish affairs.) He was able to find the kind of sponsorship that instantly gave the court financial stability and social respectability. He persuaded men like David Sarnoff to serve on the board of trustees, and was president of the organization for many years. Louis Richman served as executive director and chief spark plug until his death in 1958. (Both his functions are performed today by his widow, Ruth Richman, who took courses in social work after her marriage so that she could help her husband with his all-consuming hobby.)

Close to a thousand cases are brought to the Board every year, though only about 6 percent of them ever actually come to trial. Many are settled amicably in Mrs. Richman's office after a visit or two. Through the years the cases have fallen, by and large, into the same familiar categories—marital disputes; business disputes; disputes between members and their lodges, clubs, and societies; disputes between parents and children, brothers and sisters, friends and neighbors; disputes of a more or less religious nature among synagogue officials, rabbis, cantors, and worshipers. What has changed, and continues to change, is the relative frequency of cases in each category and some of the motives that provoke the participants.

These changes reflect the changing history of America in this last half century. In the 1920's, when the Jewish immigrant community was comparatively new, there were many more cases hinging on the interpretation of religious rituals and laws than there are today. In the 1930's the court was swamped by cases in which the chief factor was money, or rather the lack of it: bankruptcy disputes, fights over organizational dues, marital problems caused by poverty, and poignant cases in which elderly parents sued their grown children for support. To read some of these is to taste, without the sugarcoating of today's fad for nostalgia, the bitter flavor of the depression. For example, an old man's children demand that his daughter should be the only one to support him because her husband is the "rich" member of the family. As it turns out, this son-in-law *is* the richest among them; he has a WPA job and earns $50 a month.

In the postwar years, with the advent of Social Security, Medicare, and other government provisions for the elderly, there has been a sharp decrease in support cases of this kind. There has also been a sharp increase in cases in which emotional disturbance and mental illness are important elements. As America has grown more aware of such problems, so has the Jewish court. Not long ago the judges would never have thought of recommending psychiatric treatment for

*10*

litigants, but they make this recommendation often today. And Mrs. Richman keeps on hand a list of psychiatrists who will see patients from the Board at reduced fees.

All these changes have their importance. Nevertheless, the fundamental purposes of the court remain today pretty much what they were in 1920.

First, the court still deals with matters of special Jewish concern that might be incomprehensible to non-Jewish judges. Obvious examples are disagreements between individuals and their synagogues on points of ritual or protocol, cases in which wives and husbands accuse one another of violating the Sabbath or the dietary laws, problems raised by the intricacies of Jewish burial customs, cases in which old people want money from their children so they can spend their last days in Israel. (The children often refuse, not because they can't afford the money but because they feel their parents are rejecting them.) But even when a case doesn't deal specifically with religious matters, it may well contain psychological elements or involve social mores that are peculiarly and subtly Jewish.

The court's second major purpose, retaining as much force today as it ever did, is to protect the dignity of the Jewish name. Among Jews business dealings can be as ruthless, family squabbles as petty, sexual behavior as outlandish as among any other people. But Jews are particularly averse to washing this dirty linen in public; they know too well how the gentile world can use their dirty linen against them. The Board serves as a place where messy disputes that otherwise might become public in civil proceedings can be kept fairly quiet.

The third major purpose of the court has the most

relevance perhaps to the world outside the Jewish community. The court is designed to save time and money for people who cannot easily afford either. Civil courts nowadays, especially those in big cities, are notoriously overcrowded. Cases often take three or four years before they come to trial; court fees and legal expenses can mount up frighteningly. The Jewish Conciliation Board, on the other hand, charges no fees and discourages the appearance of lawyers. Cases are brought before it within a month or two after the complaint is lodged, and the judges usually render a decision on the spot, after a short consultation. This makes the Board a convenient arena even for disputes that have no special Jewish angle and could appropriately be handled by a civil court. In recent years, as a matter of fact, both Jewish and non-Jewish judges in New York civil courts have frequently tried to ease their clogged dockets by referring litigants to the Board.

The fourth purpose of the Board, present though unexpressed from the start, has emerged clearly in the course of time. The Board conceives of itself not only as a body that dispenses justice but even more as a body that tries to make peace among the disputants. The emergence of this hidden purpose is reflected by the changes in the organization's official title through the years. When Louis Richman and Rabbi Buckler founded it, it was known as the Jewish Court of Arbitration. Later it changed its name to the Jewish Board of Arbitration; the word *court* carried an implication of sternness and implacability that it wanted to avoid. Later still it arrived at its present name, the Jewish Conciliation Board, which expresses its feeling that to render an objective decision is not enough; the parties to the quarrel must also, somehow, be made happy with the decision, and ideally the case must end with them kissing and making up.

In one form or another, the judges—we will see in the next chapter who they are—are constantly stating this principle to the litigants. One judge says, "We are not going to attempt to say who is morally or legally justified; we are interested in settling things." Another judge says, "Our religious tradition teaches us that it doesn't matter who is right or wrong. There should be a sense of compassion and forgiveness." Another judge, about to deliver an extremely conciliatory decision, says, "This may be rough justice, but here it is." And when one of the litigants objects that the justice is a bit too rough, the judge tells him sternly, "In Jewish law we don't just go by the paragraph; we go beyond it." Furthermore, the judges pay much more than lip service to the ideal of conciliation. They spend a lot of time trying to achieve it in individual cases.

Popularly—in the Jewish press, for instance—the Board is still known as "the court." But this does not mean that the litigants don't share its dedication to conciliation. Many of them, in fact, seem to come to the court precisely because they want to meet their opponents halfway and don't know how to go about it. One example: Five grown sons who used to support their old widowed mother have suddenly stopped giving her any money. The old lady brings them before the court, where each son angrily accuses the others of being stingy and ungrateful. Conciliation seems to be the last thing on any of their minds. But under questioning by the judges they gradually reveal the true cause of the trouble. The sons love their mother and are able to support her, but there is great rivalry among their wives. A few months earlier one of these daughters-in-law decided that her husband earned less than the others and therefore should give less, so she made him reduce his weekly payment by fifty cents. As soon as this happened, a second daughter-in-law became afraid that it would look as if she had less wifely influence than her sister-in-law did, so she made *her* husband reduce his payment by fifty cents too. This caused a chain reaction among all five daughters-in-law, each one competing with the others to reduce the payments fifty cents at a time, until soon the old lady was getting nothing.

It is now clear to the judges that the sons (and maybe their wives too) are sick of the whole fracas and want nothing more than to start supporting the old lady again, but nobody dares to lose face by making the first move. They are begging the judges to make this move for them, to act as an impartial outside force that will compel them to yield without sacrificing their pride.

The judges are happy to oblige. *Sholom bais*—peace in the house—is the phrase most frequently to be found in the records of the court.

# CHAPTER

## 2

### Procedure

There is, of course, a procedure for the preparation and presentation of cases. Every court, however informal or unconventional, must have its official routine.

Each case begins its life with the Board in the same way, by someone coming to the executive director's office and filing a complaint. (People hear about the Board through word of mouth or through the coverage it receives in the Yiddish press. The Board does no advertising; it simply hasn't got the funds.) The office is located in an old skyscraper on lower Broadway, near the Federal and state courthouses and City Hall. The Board shares its small, rather seedy waiting room with four lawyers and a certified public accountant, none of them connected with the Board. Mrs. Richman's secretary—who must know not only how to type and take shorthand but how to do it in Yiddish—sits at a desk flanked by filing cabinets, answers the phone for the lawyers and the accountant as well as for the Board, and greets and seats a heterogeneous collection of visitors throughout the day. It is sometimes difficult to tell which of these visitors have come to see Mrs. Richman and which have come to put themselves in the hands of the more official and expensive representatives of justice.

Mrs. Richman sees the complainant and takes down his story in detail; this first interview, and very likely several subsequent interviews, becomes part of the Board's permanent files. Mrs. Richman may feel that the complaint has no substance and try to persuade the complainant to carry it no further. Or she may feel that the complainant really wants nothing except a chance to pour out his troubles into a sympathetic ear, in which case she will administer a pat on the back and an encouraging word and send him on his way. If the case seems worth following up, or if the complainant insists on doing so, Mrs. Richman's next step is to write to the prospective defendant and invite him to come in and tell his side of the story. If he agrees—and if by this time Mrs. Richman's own benevolent influence hasn't induced the hostile parties to make up their differences —the case is scheduled for the next session of the court. These sessions take place once and often twice a month so that no litigant has to wait too long.

The press and the public are permitted to attend the sessions. For over twenty-five years the proceedings of the court have been reported by *The Forward* and other Yiddish newspapers, but the reporters are pledged never to use real names.

Before the session Mrs. Richman prepares a précis of each case on the docket. The judges can study this; it is the only pretrial preparation they do. Then comes one of the most ticklish and important parts of the procedure. Each party must sign an arbitration agreement before the judges will hear the case. This is a standard form similar to that used by the NLRB in labor disputes; it states that, having voluntarily agreed to submit themselves to arbitration, the parties hereby bind themselves to accept the decision. Once both parties have signed this form, the court's decision has powerful legal teeth in it. Both the federal and state judiciary recognize the Board as a legal arbitration agency and if necessary will uphold its decisions in state supreme court without hearing any further witnesses or evidence.

The Board itself has no machinery to enforce its decisions, but the arbitration agreement usually makes enforcement unnecessary. A letter from Mrs. Richman to a reluctant party, containing a gentle allusion to the state supreme court, is enough to produce results in most cases. In a few instances this letter has failed, and the winning party has taken the losing party to the supreme court; each time the Board's decision has been affirmed. (The situation operates in reverse too, of course. On at least one occasion a husband and wife came to the Board with a domestic dispute in which a judgment had already been awarded in civil court. As soon as the judges found out about this, they refused to consider the case.)

Because the arbitration agreement is binding, the Board has from its earliest days bent over backward to make sure that nobody signs it unless they really want to. The signing takes place in the presence of Mrs. Richman, the executive director, just before the case is heard in court. No coercion is used; there is no coaxing, no special appeal. And for this reason, of course, many people get cold feet. The docket for each session invariably includes two or three cases that never actually come to trial because one party or the other has balked at signing the arbitration agreement.

To the curiosity seeker this is often a frustrating situation. We read in the files, for instance, about Lily Schwartz, age thirty-five, who has been undergoing psychiatric care for her many emotional problems. The doctor told her that these problems result from her seduction at the age of sixteen by a young man named Slotkin back in her native Poland. Last month she suddenly encountered Slotkin on the street; in fact, he is now a garment manufacturer in Brooklyn. So Lily and her brother bring him before the Board, demanding that he pay her psychiatrist bills. The human interest aspects of this case are enormous; the legal and moral implications are intriguing. But unfortunately none of these possibilities will ever lead to anything, because the vile seducer Slotkin refuses at the last moment to sign the arbitration agreement.

But let us say that the necessary documents are signed, and the case does come to trial. The courtroom is located in the Educational Alliance, that hallowed old building on the Lower East Side that has served immigrants in so many ways since the turn of the century. It is a medium-sized, totally undecorated room, with hard wooden chairs on a cheap tiled floor, long gloomy window shades, and high ceilings. This room is so overwhelmingly dreary that one almost suspects the effect of being deliberate. How many prospective litigants, seeing each other face to face in these grim surroundings, have lost heart and decided to settle their differences just for the relief of getting out of here?

Yet the truth seems to be the opposite. The sessions of the Board took place for many years in a large conventional courtroom in the Municipal Building on Madison Street; it was turned over to the Board in the late afternoon, after regular court hours. (All sessions of the Board are held in late afternoon to accommodate the working schedules of litigants and judges alike.) In the 1940's the sessions were moved to the Educational Alliance, and everybody felt happier about this. The tacky, unimposing character of the present surroundings suits the informal nature of the court much better than a standard courtroom does. And the Educational Alliance itself has a warm, reassuring effect on many of the people who come to the court; it serves as a solid reminder of the comfortable past. As one complainant put it to the judges, "I was brought up on the East Side. This place brings back a lot of memories." The judges didn't uphold his complaint, but he may well have felt better about his defeat because of where it took place.

At the front of the room, below the windows, is a long wooden table where the judges sit. It is not placed on a raised platform; no artificial awe is created by forcing the litigants to look up at the judges. In fact, it is the judges who have to look up while people pace up and down in front of the table, lean across it to shake their fingers in a judge's face, or bang their fists down for emphasis. The judges wear no long black robes and wield no gavels. If they are male, they probably wear yamalkes out of respect for the Orthodox religious feelings of many of the litigants. Otherwise their appearance is no different from anybody else's in the room.

This tall, thin, mildly smiling gentleman with the thick glasses is Everyman's absentminded scholar; this fat, triple-chinned, rather pompous little man is Everyman's business tycoon; this small, well-dressed, energetic lady in her fifties is Everyman's Jewish club woman; she comes to court a bit late, out of breath, complaining about her inept cabdriver, until one of her fellow judges says, "Don't aggravate yourself, dear, sit down and be comfortable."

But who are these judges really, and on what basis have they been chosen? There are always at least three of them, and the mix is always the same: one rabbi, one lawyer, one businessman. The rabbi can be Orthodox, Conservative, or Reform; some extremely distinguished and busy members of the rabbinate have found time to serve on the court. The lawyer may well be a judge in his normal professional life, but he certainly doesn't have to be. The businessman—a loose term that seems to designate anyone in the Jewish community who is neither a rabbi nor a lawyer—may be a manufacturer of ladies' underwear, the general manager of *The Forward*, a widow who serves prominently on charitable committees, or Harry Golden. Also present at the front table for each session is the Board's consulting psychiatrist; he serves in an advisory rather than a judicial capacity but he often participates in questioning the litigants and deliberating on the decision.

There are obvious reasons for the presence of a rabbi and a lawyer on the panel, but there are also some not so obvious reasons. The rabbi is there, of course, because he is presumably an authority on the religious tradition and can bolster his opinions with quotations from the Talmud and the Torah. But he is also there because, as a rabbi, he adds weight and prestige to the court's decisions, at least among certain people in the community. If the purpose of the court is not only to judge but to convince, it becomes a matter of importance that many people amenable to no other appeal will listen to a rabbi. The lawyer is part of the panel, obviously, because his knowledge of civil and criminal law will prevent the Board from unwittingly running afoul of some technicality and also because his courtroom experience gives him an edge in questioning witnesses and evaluating evidence. But he is also present because of his mastery of legal phraseology; he can announce decisions in long rolling sentences full of impressive technical terms; to the uneasy litigant who feels somehow that this is not a "real" court, the lawyer's language can make everything sound more legal.

And why is the third member of the panel always a businessman? Dr. Israel Goldstein says, "A lot of situations require common-sense experience, dealing with practical affairs from a nontechnical approach. The businessman can use this approach to balance and counteract the other two." Dr. Goldstein ought to know; he has many of the attributes of a successful businessman himself. Yet it also seems that the businessman is necesary to the court for a subtler reason. His "nontechnical approach" adds very little, I think, to the value of his opinions, but it does have the important effect of soothing and reassuring the litigant. The businessman's presence pulls the aura of the proceedings down to the level of the average man. He *is* the average man, in fact, and so he gives the people who make use of the court the feeling that they are being judged at least in part by somebody just like themselves. This feeling is essential if any true conciliation is to take place.

So here are the judges, here is their table, here is the room. The executive director calls for the first case, and each judge shuffles quickly through his mimeographed précis. Then the complainant comes up to the table and states his complaint—usually at length, with the judges breaking in to ask questions and make comments and sometimes with the defendant breaking in indignantly to deny lies that are being told about him. "You'll get your chance in a few minutes," say the judges, and the complainant finishes his story.

Now the judges turn to the defendant and ask for his response. He will go on at length too, and the complainant will have *his* opportunity to interrupt with denials. The judges ask more questions in an effort to straighten out the discrepancies between the stories. Then, if appropriate, they will call for witnesses; the child of an unhappy marriage, for instance, will describe his parents' arguments from a point of view that contradicts both of them. Physical evidence may be produced—a savings book that proves beyond a doubt (at least to the wife's satisfaction) that her husband has been robbing her; the constitution of a *landsmanschaft* society, painstakingly written out in Yiddish, full of contradictory clauses that seem to substantiate both sides of an argument at once. Some litigants have a very confused notion about what constitutes evidence. A widow demanding money that she claims was owed to her husband triumphantly produces a "receipt" that on examination proves to be a crumpled old piece of paper, full of smudges, with a few numbers scrawled over it and no recognizable names or signatures. The poor lady can't understand why the judges don't automatically award her the money on the strength of this document.

Sometimes most of the case is taken up not with evidence or testimony but with arguments among the hostile parties, usually on a variety of irrelevant subjects. The judges may cut off these arguments sharply, but more often they will listen to them quietly for a while. This is a good way to learn what the people are like.

Eventually the judges send the litigants out of the room and have a conference to arrive at a decision. Many points are likely to be brought up in this conference—points of common sense, of talmudic law, of practical consequences, of compassion or distrust for the warring parties. But there is one kind of point, frequent enough in conventional courts, that never gets brought up. The judges never refer to precedents based on decisions in previous cases. Each case before the court is considered on its own terms and weighed against no external, developing body of law. As a matter of fact, since the panel changes each session and no individual is likely to serve more than a few times in a year, the chances are the judges don't even know about earlier cases that might provide precedents. Yet there is a strong sense of tradition underlying their decisions —a tradition of Jewish justice, "a Jewish feeling" that will be discussed in more detail later. This tradition is powerful enough so that a judge often buttresses his decision with the same principles and arguments that were used ten years earlier by a different judge in a totally unrelated case.

The litigants are now called back to the court, and

the decision is presented to them. This part of the procedure—usually a cold formality in a conventional court—is of the utmost importance in the Jewish court. The judges take great care in the wording of their decision; the point must be made in such a way that even the losers, if possible, go off without hard feelings. Careful consideration is given to selecting which judge will announce the decision; what some people will accept only from the mouth of the rabbi, others will accept from any mouth *but* the rabbi's. There is also an effort, in the wording of the decision, to deal not only with specific issues but with the general principles they embody. The parties to a dispute must ultimately understand the moral implications of what they did.

In most cases they are willing to accept what the judges tell them. Often—especially in clashes among members of a family—the decision leads to an orgy of emotion, with everybody apologizing to everybody else and tears flowing freely, not only from the litigants but from the spectators, the reporters, and the judges. Sometimes—especially in marital disputes—the bitterness is too great to be eliminated. It is not unusual for somebody to leave the courtroom muttering angrily, making vague threats, shaking his fist.

Occasionally the judges are unable to come to a decision in one session, possibly because a key witness or an important document is missing or because an audit, an inventory, or a psychiatric examination has to be made. They will then postpone the case until the next convenient session of the court, at which time the parties will probably have to tell their stories all over again to an entirely new panel of judges. By rights this ought to cause a lot of confusion, and sometimes it does. But the amazing thing is how often the second group of judges will follow the same line of questioning and arrive at the same conclusions as the first.

And so the case is concluded, and the executive director calls for the next case. As few as two or as many as six cases may be heard in one session, lasting between three and four hours. Quite a drain on the time of three busy people with active careers. Furthermore, the judges are never paid for their work; in fact, when fund-raising time for the Board comes around, they are likely to find themselves high on the executive director's list. Why do they do it? Dr. Goldstein says that they look upon it as a mitzvah—that is, God gives you a blessing by allowing you to do a favor for your fellow man. No doubt, but it is also true that Jews love to be judges, to unravel difficult human problems, to pronounce opinions on all subjects. The reporter for *The Forward*, after describing a complicated marital case held in the court, invited his readers to write in and comment on the decision. The newspaper was swamped with letters, most of them disagreeing with the judges. Every Jew believes in his heart of hearts that he could do a better job than any of those so-called distinguished men.

It is dark outside now, time for judges, litigants, and curiosity seekers to leave the old Educational Alliance Building and go home. But many of the cases heard and settled today are far from over. Mrs. Richman and her assistants, some volunteer, some paid by the Board, may be busy for weeks or months, even for years, following up the consequences of what occurred in court. Sometimes the judges have specifically instructed her to do so—by referring the parties to a marriage counselor, a psychiatrist, or an accountant, all of whom it is Mrs. Richman's job to provide. But even without specific instructions she will continue the Board's involvement in a case whenever this seems appropriate. She will ask the parties to keep in touch with her and tell her how they're getting along—and they often do, especially if an emergency arises.

The records of the Board are full of examples of its posttrial activities. Some years ago a family was engaged in a complicated dispute over their late father's savings; after the hearing, Louis Richman went down to the savings bank with all the parties and supervised the division of the money into separate accounts. On another occasion an old lady had been advised by the court to apply for welfare; Louis Richman filled out and sent in her application, and when the Department of Welfare awarded her only $28 a month, he wrote a letter to the welfare commissioner explaining the details of the case and requesting a raise in the allotment.

More recently, a sixteen-year-old girl, just orphaned, was brought before the court by the aunt who had taken her in to live. The aunt accused her of being fresh and lazy, doing poorly at school, staying out too late at night. The judges could do nothing except to suggest that both parties should be tolerant and adjust to each other; the real work on the case began later, when Mrs. Richman found a room with a congenial family for the girl to move into, talked to her teachers about her grades, got her a part-time job after school, worked out a budget for her, even advised her on what clothes to wear and how to do her hair.

One case in particular shows how far the Board and its executive director will go in order to carry out the wishes of the court. Mr. Beltz, a butcher, is suddenly left a widower at the age of forty-seven. He has two girls of twelve and eight, who go to live with his wife's mother, Mrs. Shapiro; Beltz doesn't live there, but eats his meals there and spends every weekend with the girls. The situation has become intolerable to him, and he brings his mother-in-law before the court, demanding that the children should leave her and go to live with his married sister. In the hearing, he explains his reasons: "I said to the old lady that when I come to her home I don't want her to eat me up alive. I work hard as a butcher, eight, ten, fourteen hours a day. I have Saturday for myself. If I want to take them out, she says no. She curses my sister so that the children don't know how to act with my family. She talks to people about the children, and I don't want that."

Mrs. Shapiro defends herself. She says that he never takes the children out for recreation. Instead he takes them to his sister. "She speaks hatefully about their mother, and the children dislike her for it. She always quarreled with their mother. Once Mr. Beltz came up to my house and a disagreement developed over the children and his family. We pushed each other in the excitement and the police was called."

The judges take the view that what matters most is the children's welfare. "The core of this great tragedy is the children. You cannot throw them around like a bag of potatoes." The court psychiatrist has spoken with the children before the hearing, and he gives his opinion that they have a good relationship with their grandmother. He recommends that they stay with her. The judges feel sympathy for Beltz, but they confirm the psychiatrist's opinion—the children will stay with their grandmother, and Beltz is ordered to continue paying what he has been paying, $42.50 a week, toward their rent and expenses.

That would seem to be that, but Mrs. Richman takes seriously the underlying idea of the court's decision, that the welfare of the children is what matters. From her point of view, these children have now become unofficial wards of the Board. So she keeps in touch with their grandmother, and seven months after the hearing she learns that Beltz has stopped his weekly contribution and refuses to help buy the girls more clothing. Mrs. Richman writes him one of her sweet, subtly threatening letters, bringing in almost casually the name of the state supreme court. Shortly afterward Beltz resumes his weekly contributions.

Two months later Mrs. Shapiro has more complaints. She has sent the children to summer camp, and Beltz refuses to pay more than half the bill. Further, using this camp bill as a justification, he has cut his weekly contribution down to $40. Mrs. Richman talks with Mrs. Shapiro at length and begins to sense that her complaints against Beltz are only distractions from what's really bothering her. She is old, she is worn out, she needs help with the children; she loves them but she is becoming uncertain that she can take care of them all by herself.

Mrs. Richman asks Beltz to come into the office, hoping she can persuade him not only to restore his weekly contribution to its old level but to increase it so that Mrs. Shapiro can afford to hire some help. Beltz insists that he can't afford any more, and he proves it to Mrs. Richman. Business is less good than it was; he makes only $100 a week now. After paying his rent, utilities, phone, carfare, taxes, and giving Mrs. Shapiro $40 a week—less than what the judges ordered him to give— he has only $45 a month left. And Mrs. Shapiro is constantly after him for extras—clothes, camps, music lessons—does she think he's made of money? He complains also that he can't afford to take the girls out on Saturdays, so he wants them to visit him in his apartment, but whenever he asks them, they say they're too busy. He knows perfectly well that Mrs. Shapiro influences them to say that. And one more thing—he wishes to remarry, he has even met somebody, but he dares not do it because it would cost too much.

The situation looks impossible, but Mrs. Richman gets in touch with the Welfare Department and gets information about the law on grandmothers supporting grandchildren. She uncovers a technicality that adds a small amount every month to Mrs. Shapiro's income— enough to calm the old lady down for a while. Mrs. Richman also arranges for Mrs. Shapiro to go once a week to a free counseling service; she hopes they can give the old lady some temporary peace of mind that will make it easier for her to be with the children.

Ten months later a disaster strikes Mrs. Shapiro, which she immediately brings to Mrs. Richman's attention. The law has been changed, and Welfare has dropped its payments. Mrs. Shapiro is in despair; she inveighs against Welfare, she has a whole new cluster of complaints against Beltz, her arm is in a sling as a result of a fall, she has bad arthritis, the children are getting harder and harder to handle, she is sixty-eight years old and needs more money; she wants Mrs. Richman to make Beltz increase his contribution. Once again Mrs. Richman detects the underlying complaint, the words that the old lady can't bring herself to say, and to stave off these words, to keep the old lady from committing herself to them openly and therefore irrevocably, Mrs. Richman calls Beltz, makes a strong appeal, and actually levers an extra $8.00 a month out of him.

But she knows that the crisis has only been postponed. Three months later Mrs. Shapiro comes in again. (She is becoming dependent on the Board for advice and hand-holding, a not unfamiliar phenomenon among older clients.) She says that Beltz is still paying every week, but he accompanies his money with curses over the phone. Mrs. Richman advises her to ignore the curses, but the old lady insists that she wants another hearing before the court. Ostensibly this is to stop Beltz from cursing her, but Mrs. Richman fears that the old lady hopes for a different result altogether.

Nevertheless, the new hearing must be held. Meanwhile, just to check her own diagnosis, Mrs. Richman gets in touch with the counseling service that has been seeing Mrs. Shapiro. They confirm what Mrs. Richman has suspected—the old lady is extremely ambivalent about the children; she loves them but feels impelled to wash her hands of them; she wants to give them up, but just as strongly she wants to keep them with her.

The second hearing is held. Before a new panel of judges all the charges and countercharges are hashed through again, almost in the same language as the first time. Beltz complains, "They come to see me only when they need money. They are not my children. They are her children. My daughter had a one hundred three temperature. She didn't even call me, but she sent me the doctor bill to pay. She made me sick. I have diabetes from her. The doctor told me the aggravation can kill me. I'll be a dead man." The judges ask him if he will further increase his contributions for the children, and he answers furiously, "I can't afford to give as much as I'm giving. I'm forty-nine years old, I'd like to get married again someday. I'm not going to rob a bank for her. Why does she always talk against me to them?"

Two things come out of this hearing. The judges work on Beltz for a long time, flattering him, cajoling him, appealing to his vanity and to his conscience, and finally they persuade him to add yet another $8.oo to his monthly contribution. This extra money partly allays the old lady's fears, but, even more important, the sight of Beltz right before her eyes, the words he speaks, his angry, whining, despairing tone of voice reinforce her conviction that she must be the one who takes care of her dead daughter's children. And so she doesn't say what Mrs. Richman was afraid she might say, and once again the case is closed.

Not really, of course. All the original exacerbations remain—there isn't enough money, the father and grandmother resent each other deeply, nobody can ever soothe their feelings. But what the Board and Mrs. Richman *can* do is keep maneuvering, keep improvising, keep putting the pressure on both parties in order to achieve the most important result: Somehow those two little girls must be got through school, through their perilous childhood, and out into the world before everything collapses around them.

# CHAPTER

# 3

## Conciliation

No step-by-step account of the court's procedure can really convey what happens when a case is heard. The true nature of the court cannot be separated from its tone, from the atmosphere it creates.

To begin with, the manner of the court is almost aggressively informal. This is part of a deliberate effort to avoid the stiffness and sternness of the conventional court; people cannot be conciliated and intimidated at the same time. The judges don't look or dress like judges, and they also make a point of not sounding like judges. In talking to the litigants they cultivate an easy, relaxed tone. They frequently open a case by saying, "The judges are your friends; there is no red tape here." They soon prove it. One judge interrupts a lady's testimony to ask, "May someone know how old you are?" The lady answers, with a blush, "Why not? I am almost forty." The judge says gallantly, "You don't look it." Another judge says to a complaining husband, "You must realize that you are not perfect." The husband says, with a shrug, "Nobody is perfect. Even Professor Einstein wasn't perfect." The judge shoots back, "Don't overdo it," and the spectators obligingly laugh. Another judge engages in this bit of snappy repartee with one of the litigants:

|  |  |
|---|---|
| JUDGE: | What is your problem? |
| MR. SAMUELS: | I have no problem. |
| JUDGE: | Are you happy? |
| MR. SAMUELS: | No. |
| JUDGE: | Then you have a problem. |

There are moments when we feel as if we are less in the world of Blackstone or Moses than in the world of the late Bobby Clark.

To further sustain the tone of informality, the judges never hesitate to bring their own lives, families, and personal problems into a case. They try to put the litigant at ease and in a receptive frame of mind for their advice by letting him know that they have been in the same boat that he is in. A wife complains that her husband never gives her any presents, and the husband answers that he doesn't know what she likes. The judge says, "I am also guilty of this same thing. I would rather give my wife money and let her buy what she wants. A lot of men are this way." A judge lectures a neglectful wife, "Do you know how much it means to me when my wife compliments me? It is worth more than all the millions in the world." To a distraught husband who can't forgive his wife for an affair she had before their marriage, the judge says, "When you marry you start a new life. I was divorced and I am now married again. My wife was a widow, and she had children and so did I. What I am trying to bring out is that whatever happened between my former wife and me, and her former husband and her, is never discussed. We have a policy that we never discuss our former mates, and it is a healthy and good relationship."

As this last example indicates, judges sometimes get carried away and go on a bit too long. How many of us could resist the temptation of telling our life stories to a captive audience? And a note of self-satisfaction does have a way of creeping in. Nevertheless, these defects seem to be outweighed by the genuinely homey and reassuring atmosphere that is created.

It isn't just talk that creates this atmosphere. The judges are always willing to bend or stretch or even ignore their own rules and regulations when their deeper purposes require it. Complainants are supposed to present their cases ahead of defendants—but is this written on some sacred scroll? Mr. Blitz says, "Could my wife start?" The judge says, "You speak first, you made the complaint." Mr. Blitz says, "Let her start. She is angrier with me than I am with her." And the judges agree to this change in order. Often a litigant can't appear in court because he is too old or too sick or gets called out of town on business. In such cases, if it's all right with both parties, the judges will allow the litigant's wife or son or best friend or any other representative to speak for him.

Belief in the value of informality is what accounts for the adverse reaction of the judges when litigants are accompanied by their lawyers. Mrs. Gelb brings a lawyer to the hearing of her charges against her husband,

and the judges become disturbed. "This is very unusual," one of them says. "While we don't absolutely prohibit it, we don't encourage it either. Our tribunal is not merely to render a decision but rather to create an atmosphere in which you will be able to live in peace. Now that Mrs. Gelb has showed up with a lawyer, Mr. Gelb is upset, and this lessens the amount of *sholom* that will flow from this meeting."

Informality also has its dangers. Many of the litigants, noticing the easygoing manner in which the judges treat them, are not slow to reply in kind. The records of the court are full of remarks and actions from litigants that would get them cited for contempt in any other court. A complainant refuses to let anybody get a word in edgewise; he keeps jumping to his feet, interrupting, shouting. Finally the judge puts in dryly, "I have been trying to say something for some time." The complainant gives a gracious wave of his hand: "All right, what do you want to say?" An obstreperous lady, asked to explain her charges, launches into the story of her life from twenty years before. The judge breaks in, "Can't you come up to the beginning of this year?" She says, "I have to tell you everything. All I want is to talk for ten minutes." And she goes on with nobody daring to stop her. Another lady begins her story by telling the judges how brilliant her children have always been. They are grown up now, and they have nothing to do with her case anyway, but nevertheless she pulls out a bundle of their old report cards and proceeds to summarize them in detail.

This excess of informality sometimes gets on the the judges' nerves and prompts them to snap at the litigants. "We don't want to be interrupted! I think this

35

court is entitled to a little respect! We do not recognize your claim; we have the right to decide and we've decided, so keep quiet already!" Out of this particular case not much conciliation is likely to come—judges are only human too.

The miracle is that they lose their tempers so infrequently, that they maintain their patient conciliatory tone under such brutal assaults. But from the beginning of a case to its end, they almost always do.

To promote the spirit of conciliation there is one simple technique that the judges often use. If possible, the litigants must be given an opportunity to arrive at their own decision rather than have a decision imposed on them from the outside. A classic illustration is the case of Samuel Vorspan, the beneficiary of his late father's $2500 insurance policy. Vorspan's old and indigent mother wants him to give her a part of this money; the judges realize that they have a right to compel him, but they hope to avoid this extreme remedy. In the courtroom Vorspan resists all persuasion; the judges still don't give up. They postpone their final decision and get Vorspan to agree to meet Louis Richman in the Board's office "for further discussion." Richman goes through all the arguments over again with Vorspan, who hesitates, agrees to think it over, goes away, calls up to say no, agrees to think it over some more, and finally after a week breaks down and offers to give his mother $1000. As soon as his check clears, the judges announce their official decision—that Mr. Vorspan is to give his mother $1000.

The same technique is used in the case of an old man, Mr. Kleiner, who has worked for twelve years as a night watchman at a small hospital for the aged. The executive director of the hospital, Mr. Saperstein, has just fired Kleiner on the grounds of incompetence and given him the legal two weeks' separation pay. Kleiner thinks he is entitled to a lot more money, but Saperstein is adamant. He brings out a long list of Kleiner's inadequacies; he feels he should have fired the man years ago but didn't because he felt sorry for him; therefore, when the judges appeal to his kindness of heart, his answer is that his kindness of heart has already stretched over twelve years. "I was a prisoner too long, so enough is enough."

The judges wear Saperstein down by attacking him on three fronts. First, they make a logical point designed to appeal to his businesslike side. "You are not supposed to keep a man who is incompetent, but when such a man has been with you for twelve years, you condoned his incompetency; like a wife may be unfaithful but the husband keeps on living with her, he condones her guilt." Then they appeal to his conscience: "The man has been with you twelve years, Mr. Saperstein. Whatever he is, doesn't that count for something? From the humanitarian angle, not the legal, do you really think those two weeks' pay are adequate?" And finally they appeal to his pride by giving him the chance to make a generous gesture of his own free will: "Injury has been done to him—now what do you think would be fair for the home to give him?"

"You mean from *my* pocket," Saperstein says, "because as far as the home is concerned, we are not Federation."

Saperstein has given vent to his sense of injury, so now he can let his pride win out. He offers old Kleiner an extra two months' pay.

Instantly the judges are all over Saperstein with compliments and praises. "We are delighted whenever we adjudicate these things by voluntary tactics," says one of the judges. "It is lovely of Mr. Saperstein to voluntarily agree to give Mr. Kleiner this additional compensation. He is doing a fine thing. We appreciate the magnanimous manner in which Mr. Saperstein has handled himself."

"Voluntary tactics" won't succeed every time. There are many cases in which the judges ask the disputants to go into another room and work out their own compromise; more often than not, they return to say that they haven't been able to work out anything. But it seems clear that the very act of trying and failing must make them a bit more willing to accept the court's compromise; the feeling that they are free is often more important to men than the actual exercise of their freedom.

And whether the decision has been arrived at voluntarily or not, the judges are always careful to include in that decision a large measure of flattery. Over and over they will say to the litigants, both the winners and the losers, "You are very fine people," "You are a very nice couple," "You are running an extremely worthwhile organization." The effect of this is sometimes unintentionally comic—for the "very nice couple" may well have revealed themselves, in the course of the testimony, to be a prize pair of selfcentered childish idiots, and the "extremely worthwhile organization" may have been convicted by these same flattering judges of outrageously greedy and ruthless behavior.

For instance, the court hears the case of an old cantor whose synagogue promised him $100 if the attendance at high holidays went above a certain number. It did go above that number but the officers of the synagogue simply refused to give the old man his money. A clearcut case of chiseling, and the judges find in the cantor's favor, but they are careful to include the following fulsome paragraph in their official decision: "All of us want to tell you that your community is fortunate indeed to have the kind of leadership you have given to this congregation. The congregation deserves to be congratulated for having officers of your caliber."

Hypocrisy perhaps, but surely in a good cause. The old cantor, after all, must go on earning his bread from those synagogue officers. Conciliation is a practical as well as a spiritual idea.

# CHAPTER

# 4

❧ ❧
❧

# *Decision*

Not every case achieves even this measure of success. Some people are conciliation-proof. In many cases conciliation would be beside the point; a definite decision is required. With all their dedication to conciliation the judges have never been tempted to use it as a pious substitute for taking a stand. When called upon for a decision, they will deliver one, though it will often be very different from what we might expect to encounter in a conventional court.

What characterizes many of their most interesting decisions is a paradoxical mixture of pragmatism with idealism, toughness with compassion, strict adherence to law and logic with a romantic conviction that truth can be found only if law and logic are transcended. This mixture is typically if not exclusively Jewish; it pervades the Talmud, that great collection of biblical commentaries that provides the basis for Jewish law and much Jewish custom.

One of the first things we notice about the court's decisions is how often the judges justify them by quoting, or misquoting, from the Talmud. Sometimes they do this in passing, just to give rhetorical emphasis to a point they are making. "Under no circumstances," says a judge to a husband accused of cursing his wife, "are you to utter a curse. The Talmud tells us that this is not a sin against the other person but a sin against God." Sometimes the words of the Talmud become the very basis of the final decision. A group of people from the same village in Poland, who are all survivors of the Nazis, publish a book to commemorate those from their village who were killed; they distribute this book privately among friends and family. In this book they recount certain unflattering, reprehensible facts about several of the dead. The surviving relatives complain to the Board; the writers of the book defend themselves on the grounds that the facts are true and everyone knows it. In sustaining the complaint the Board's rabbi says, "Even if what you wrote is true, the Talmud forbids us to publish anything bad about a dead person, especially a martyr. Rebbe Gershom says that one may be excommunicated from his people for this." A formula for a public apology is worked out, and the writers of the book are ordered to print copies of this apology, include one in every subsequent mailing of the book, and send one to every person who has already received a book.

Do these examples suggest, then, that the court is really a legalistic body whose decisions are rigorously based on an ancient code of law? It isn't quite that simple. Take the case of Noah Fleischer, whose father gave a Torah to his synagogue before he died. Now, twenty-five years later, the congregation is talking about dissolving itself, and Fleischer wants his father's Torah back. The congregation wants to sell the Torah as part of its assets, contends that it belongs to them and they can do whatever they please with it. The court's rabbi delivers the decision: "If you pledge a Torah to a synagogue, then according to the Talmud you cannot take it back unless the synagogue offers it to you. However, the synagogue cannot sell it—unless they do so for a poor girl who needs funds for her dowry—and we have no evidence to suggest that such a girl is involved in this case. On the other hand, if the synagogue is in fact dissolving, you have the right to take the Torah back."

Such are the words of the Talmud, and the conclusion would seem to be clear: Fleischer must be given the Torah, to dispose of as he sees fit. But this is not the conclusion the judges draw. They decide that the Torah will be sent to a synagogue in Israel as a donation in the name of Noah Fleischer's father; in this way the intentions of the man who bought the Torah in the first place will be carried out. This decision has a certain lovely justice about it, but what has it got to do with the Talmudic principle that the rabbi so carefully elucidated?

The answer is that the judges' view of the Talmud, like their view of everything else, is capable of adjusting itself to specific circumstances. The Talmud is, of course, the wisest book ever written, but it was, after all, written by human beings. God wants us to *use* the creations of human beings, not to *be* used by them.

42

The same flexibility applies to another, quite different attitude that seems to underline the actions of the
court. Many people believe that the court's approach is
completely down-to-earth, pragmatic. It is committed
to doing rather than theorizing. The judges never hesitate to cut the Gordian knot by taking action where
another group of judges might feel compelled to go on
talking endlessly. There is plenty of evidence to support this view of the court.

Mr. Pincus, a member of a *landsmanschaft* society,
is a persistent troublemaker. In 1958 he brings the
president of the society, Mr. Abelson, to the court. The
society, says Pincus, planned a banquet, but they were
afraid of losing money on it; so the president, Abelson,
promised that, if the deficit from the banquet went
over $200, he would contribute the difference himself.
The banquet was held; Pincus investigated and found
that the deficit was $500. "So I went to Abelson and
reminded him of his promise. He answered that his
children come first. At the next meeting I reminded
him again, and he said that he wouldn't go on being
president if I was allowed to come to the meetings."

The judge asks an obvious question: "How did the
other members feel?"

Pincus answers, "This is why we have people like
James Hoffa, because of people like the other members."

"Maybe so," says the judge, "but I am still interested
in finding out if you represent anyone else from the
society or only yourself."

"It doesn't matter," Pincus says. "I am doing this for
the good of everyone."

Abelson defends himself. He declares that he never

promised to make up the deficit. This is strictly in Pincus's imagination he says. In the minutes of the meeting at which the promise was supposed to have been made, there is no record of it. He brings a string of witnesses who attended that meeting; none of them heard him make such a promise. He points out that Pincus can't come up with *anybody* who heard this promise except himself. The judges are impressed and throw Pincus's case out of court.

Three years later, in 1961, Pincus is back; once again he has brought Abelson up on charges. Abelson is still president of the society. They have just held another banquet, and there is a deficit, and Abelson promised to make it good out of his own pocket—so Pincus wants to know where the money is. None of the judges were present for the earlier case, but Abelson wearily reminds them of it and insists once again that he never made such a promise and that nobody except Pincus accuses him of doing so. Once again the judges throw out Pincus's charges.

Two years later he is back for the third time. Abelson is no longer president; the former treasurer, Poplinsky, has taken over. The society has just held one of its perennial banquets, and according to Pincus, Poplinsky promised to make up the deficit. The judges have been provided by the executive director with summaries of Pincus's two earlier cases. When Poplinsky presents the same defense that Abelson did, the judges not only throw out the charges but also add a special clause to their decision, to the effect that Pincus shall never bring in any *future* complaints against the society and if he does the court will automatically refuse to hear them. Pincus objects indignantly to this injustice; isn't

*44*

a man always entitled to his day in court? No doubt he is; the Talmud itself probably says so. But the judges are less interested in maintaining this great abstract principle than they are in getting Pincus off the society's and the Board's backs.

And so the real motivation of the court would seem to be action at any cost and let the theories fall where they may. Yet this simple explanation is constantly being undermined too. We might think, for instance, that practical men with a solid respect for facts would give a lot of weight to concrete evidence and avoid going off half-cocked when evidence is lacking. In case after case, however, we see the judges rendering decisions, even giving away money, on the basis of no evidence at all. In these cases they are not simply being obtuse, like the lady who believed fervently in her smudged "receipt." What they are doing, quite baldly, is putting an abstraction, an ideal, above any strict adherence to facts.

An old man claims he went into a bakery, bought some cake, and gave a $50 bill to the baker; while waiting for his change he had a heart attack and was taken away in an ambulance. Now he has recovered and wants his change back from the $50. The baker says he never got the $50 bill. There is no real evidence on either side; a conventional court would have no choice but to dismiss the old man's claim. But not the judges of this court. They award the old man $25, with the following explanation: "This is not to imply in any way that the defendant took the money or that he is a liar. This is a compromise verdict. We feel that justice will be done if the complainant receives half the amount." A revealing choice of words, for "justice" is somehow seen as being done without reference to any objective considerations of evidence.

Mr. Glass, a tailor, gives his sister and brother-in-law, Mr. and Mrs. Weintraub, some cash to put in their safe-deposit box. Obviously he is trying to avoid reporting this cash to the Internal Revenue Service. But the scheme backfires. When Glass asks for his money back —$2000, he says—the Weintraubs say that he gave them only $1000. There are no records, no receipts; the judges cannot determine if the claim is genuine. Nevertheless they impose a decision on the two parties: Glass will have to live with his $1000 loss, and the Weintraubs are ordered to donate $500 to the United Jewish Appeal in Glass's name. "Sharing this loss," the judge says, "should not only symbolize the reunion of this family but also remind you of the stupidity and immorality involved in evading the law."

This case suggests what may be the most pervasive paradox in the court's approach to justice. The judges can be very tough. Glass and the Weintraubs are made to pay through the nose for their dishonesty. At the same time, the old Jewish tradition of charity, of compassion for the weak, goes hand in hand with the toughness; the United Jewish Appeal, which was never a party to the case, becomes its chief beneficiary. This strange union between toughness and compassion, sternness and warmth, underlies many of the court's decisions. It is difficult to generalize about it, though, because the mixture tends to be a little different in each individual case.

Mrs. Brenner buries her husband in the Family Circle Society plot. The dues that Mr. Brenner had paid for years entitled his wife to put up a headstone in his memory. The Family Circle says that this headstone is two inches higher than the other stones around it. They request Mrs. Brenner to have it cut down; she ignores the request, so they go ahead and cut it down themselves. She asks the court to order them to restore her husband's headstone to its original size. The Family Circle produces its constitution. There is a bylaw, clearly phrased and printed, that limits the size of headstones; Mrs. Brenner's was indeed two inches too high. This seems like a conclusive case, yet the judges don't want to leave it at that. Their sympathies are with Mrs. Brenner; they would like to decide in her favor. So they pore over the constitution and finally find another bylaw stating that the Family Circle must ask each member for a blueprint before the member is permitted to put up a headstone. It is determined that the officers never asked Mrs. Brenner for such a blueprint; in fact, it has been years since they asked *anyone* for a blueprint. Nevertheless, the judges hold the Family Circle to the technicality and order the headstone restored.

Toughness and legality have been reaffirmed, yet somehow this has also turned out to be a triumph for the underdog.

The court succeeds in bringing off another such impossible triumph in the case of Mr. Berenfeld, who was once a cantor in a synagogue but is now old, poor, and unable to sing. Twenty-eight years earlier, when the congregation was short of money, they persuaded Berenfeld to take a drastic cut in salary; in return they promised to give him $1000 as soon as the synagogue was sold to the city. (The city was widening the streets, and there were rumors that it planned to buy all the adjoining property.) But the city changed its mind, Berenfeld moved to another synagogue, the whole matter was forgotten. Only one trace of it remained— the congregation had put the promise in writing; this document had been signed by the officers and was in Berenfeld's possession.

Now, twenty-eight years later, the city has finally condemned the property and bought the synagogue in order to build an express highway. Suddenly, to the astonishment of the officers, old Berenfeld appears with his contract and demands his $1000. They refuse to give it to him, and so he has brought them to court.

A perfect case for compromise, it would seem. Surely both parties have a certain amount of right on their side. The contract *was* signed; on the other hand, the synagogue has changed hands since then, and none of its present officers signed the contract. But Berenfeld is old and sick, and it is clear that the judges want him to get his money. So all of a sudden they become the toughest, most uncompromising exponents of the letter of the law.

"For twenty-eight years this whole thing has been buried," says Bloch, the president of the synagogue.

"This contract was made, however," says the judge.

"Yes, but without the intent that it should carry over for twenty-eight years. Since that time we've built a new building and amalgamated with another synagogue. We don't even have the same name anymore."

"The new synagogue takes over the obligation."

"If it's legitimate."

"Why not legitimate? You made a contract."

"Twenty-eight years ago!"

"You can't let the date interfere," says the judge. "You made this in good faith. You made a contract."

"It was never intended to work out this way."

"You never should have made it."

"I didn't make it," Bloch cries. "I wasn't president then! I wasn't even *in* the congregation!"

"Let us not get excited," says the rabbi-judge soothingly. "This was signed by the president of your congregation. It says clearly that the money is to be paid when the synagogue is taken over for public use. Just because this didn't happen till a month ago, how does that change anything?"

"Rabbi, please—are you telling me that you really think this was made with the intent of what would happen in twenty-eight years?"

"What I think is of no importance. I only know what it says in the contract."

Bloch gets a sudden bright idea. "He left the synagogue a few years later. When his employment ended, this contract was voided."

"This is not stated," says the rabbi. "Let us hear from our lawyer on this."

The lawyer-judge frowns at the contract for about half a minute, then says, "There is no doubt in my mind that this contract is valid."

Bloch is desperate by now. "What about a compromise? Two months ago I offered him $150 to forget the whole thing. Suppose I raise that to $300?"

"Excuse me," says the rabbi, "but $1000 is what it says in the contract."

So old Berenfeld gets his $1000, and the judges have

proved to their own satisfaction what hard-boiled characters they are.

There are, furthermore, a large number of cases every year in which the judges give genuine practical help, as well as decisions and advice. A daughter has been taking care of her mother for years, but now it is time for the old lady to go into an old-age home. None of her children know how to go about this, so the court's rabbi volunteers: "My influence is great in certain places in this city. I will make an effort to obtain admission of your mother into a home." An old man complains that he can't eat the food at his old-age home. One of the judges turns out to be a trustee of that home, so he promises to go there the next night, have dinner, and find out if the old man's complaints are justified. A cutter who worked twenty years for a garment manufacturer lost his job when he became crippled in an auto accident. One of the judges, a friend of the garment manufacturer, writes him a note asking him as a personal favor to take on his old employee again.

One kind of case in particular brings out better than any other the mixture of shrewdness and tenderness that characterizes this court. Every year a few complainants appear whose charges are based on pure paranoia, totally groundless fears and anxieties that may be caused by old age, mental disturbance, or recent grief. The judges treat such cases with care and seriousness; they will expend as much energy, time, and emotion to dispel a delusion as they would to straighten out the most involuted marital or financial problem. Some of their most creative decisions are given where, strictly speaking, there was no real case in the first place.

Mrs. Hurwitz comes to court because her husband,

who is angry at her, has stopped giving her his usual thirty dollars a week to run the household. She is obliged to take the money out of their joint bank account, which is precisely where he used to get it from. In their private deliberations the judges are amused at this situation. In their official decision, however—feeling that Mrs. Hurwitz's pride must be saved, though her financial condition is in no danger—they gravely order her husband to resume payment of her thirty dollars a week.

Mrs. Ehrlich, who has never quite recovered from her nervous breakdown, is upset because her husband made her sign some papers and she doesn't know what they are. She is positive that she signed away some stocks she owns, even though the certificates are still in her possession and she never put her name on them. Her husband and children have been unable to convince her that what she signed was a routine tax form, so the judges concoct a decision to make her happy. They draw up an impressive official-looking document in which her husband swears that he never asked her to sign anything that would deprive her of her stocks; "*if* such a paper was signed, I hereby declare it null and void and without any force or effect, and I hereby cancel any agreement or writing heretofore signed by her, if such be in existence." Much relieved, Mrs. Ehrlich leaves the court, clutching this document with its "herebys" and "heretofores" that will somehow protect her against her enemies.

Old Mrs. Unger, a widow living alone, insists that her son Moe borrowed $900 from her ten years ago and now refuses to return it. Moe proves to the court that he owes his mother nothing—"she has hardening of the arteries in the head, and she forgets." The judges learn that he has been giving a $50 per month allowance to the old lady for years. So, to relieve her anxiety, they "order" her son to pay her $50 a month until the $900 he "owes" her has been returned.

# CHAPTER

# 5

## Prestige

To many observers the most astounding thing about the court is that it exists at all. How can such an institution possibly have been going on for more than fifty years, attracting thousands of potential litigants, hearing and settling scores of cases?

The court's continuing vigor and its considerable prestige are attested to by more than statistics. We have seen that the Board does no advertising; the coverage from the Yiddish press is the only form of publicity it receives. Yet many people come to it who don't read Yiddish. They come because they have been advised to come by somebody else. On each transcript in the files Mrs. Richman puts a notation about how the parties happened to hear about the Board. The notation "through *The Forward*" occurs most frequently, but "through a friend" is a close second.

And a third notation, also fairly common, is "been

here before." The court has a lot of satisfied customers who not only spread the word but keep returning themselves. One young couple with a marital problem explained to Ruth Richman what brought them to her. They were on a park bench having a spat when an elderly woman who was sitting nearby came up to them and said, "I will be an angel for you. Go to the Jewish Conciliation Board. They have helped me many times and they will help you too."

Some people come to the court filled with a sense of their rightness and prepared to challenge any opinon that disagrees with their own. But other people come in a spirit of genuine humility, puzzled over what is right and wrong, confidently expecting the judges to tell them. Such people seem less to be litigants than suppliants, children who have come to their father or teacher for advice. Businessmen unwilling to trust their employees, their customers, or their relatives trust the court.

The trust people have in the court is so great that it often remains intact even in those who feel they have been dealt with unjustly. A disgruntled wife writes to Mrs. Richman after the hearing of her marital dispute: "I have to tell you all this as you and the rest present last night were under the impression my husband was such a wonderful man. Yes, unto himself. I am wondering why your psychiatrist refused to listen to me when I said my husband was a mentally disturbed person. I am wondering why your judges were willing to pay attention to his words and not to mine." Her indictment of the court goes on, and at the end of her letter she writes, "I want to take this opportunity of thanking you and your organization for the good work you are doing, and am enclosing a $5.00 donation." This kind of ambivalent reaction is not unusual; Mrs. Richman receives several similar letters every year.

Every year there are litigants who are so impressed by the court that they come there even against their own best interests. In the middle of the high holidays, the officers of a synagogue fire a substitute cantor because the president and his wife don't like his voice. They make no attempt to pay the cantor what they owe him, so he brings them before the court. But why do they respond to his summons? Clearly he is much too poor to sue them in a regular civil court. All they have to do is sit tight, and they need not lose a cent. Even so, they sign the arbitration agreement and appear voluntarily to defend what they must know is a losing case.

The most conclusive evidence of the court's prestige is provided by the cases—there are hundreds of them every year—that never get to the judges at all because a simple reminder of the court's existence, the merest hint that the judges are waiting, is enough to force a settlement. A burial society has paid a firm of monument makers to remove stone benches from the old cemetery and transfer them to the new cemetery; after a year's delay the monument makers admit that their workmen have misplaced the benches, but they refuse to pay for the loss. They get a letter of invitation from the Board, and shortly afterward they find the missing benches and set them up in the new cemetery.

Even the people who don't back down so quickly will often be impressed and intimidated when they find themselves actually facing the judges. Before his old mother can come out with a word of her charges, a son signs an agreement to contribute to her support; just by looking at those judges he seems to know exactly what they will say to him. Another son's old parents, who are constantly fighting, would live in peace if only they had some more money, which their son refuses to give them. "I don't think you would want to see your parents separated," says one of the judges. "It might be the best thing for them," says the son. "Do you want one of them to move in with you?" says the judge, in his mildest tone of voice. Visions of what the court, with its power and influence, might do to him rise up in the son's mind. Rather quickly he comes across with the support money.

With no subpeona power, no official status, no means of compelling anyone to come before it, why should the court carry so much weight? The explanation, I think, is that the court has its roots and its present life within a community that, even after fifty years of change and assimilation, is still comparatively self-sufficient and isolated from the outside world. The court was originally founded to perform a necessary service in the lives of a distinct immigrant group that, like most immigrant groups, distrusted the civil courts. These people spoke English badly, if at all; they were uncomfortable with American customs; they were bound by Jewish taboos, rituals, values, and morals that few outsiders could hope to understand; and they had the common belief, ingrained in them in the old country, that no Jew could ever receive justice from a gentile. Throughout the 1920's and 1930's, despite much defection into the "outside world," enough of these old immigrants remained, and passed on their feelings to their children, to keep the court busy. After World War II the solidity and isolation of this community were breaking down fast; in the ordinary course of events it should have disappeared completely. But suddenly it was replenished by refugees from Europe, mostly from the Eastern countries, men, women, and children who had survived the Nazi holocaust and had no homes to return to. This group, though small indeed compared to the six million who were killed, was large enough to give new life to the court. In the last twenty years or so the community has been added to by refugees from the Soviet Union, the satellite countries, the Middle East, and Cuba.

The existence of such a community is the one essential condition for this type of court's survival. Occasionally in the past similar courts have been set up in other cities in the United States, sometimes with the advice and assistance of the Jewish Conciliation Board. So far none of them has been able to keep going for long. There are plenty of Jews in those other cities, but not enough of the type who are prepared, by training and attitude and their relation to American society, to make use of a Jewish court. (There *are* several courts, notably one in Boston, that are purely rabbinical and serve more specific and theological purposes.)

These people have certain superficial traits in common. With rare exceptions they have modest incomes, and many of them are poor, probably the poorest Jews in America. The elderly among them often live partly or wholly on Social Security, and a sizable minority of the others are receiving welfare payments. They work as butchers, bakers, barbers, waiters, night watchmen, cabdrivers, the kind of jobs that most American Jews, in their drive out of the ghetto, have gone far beyond. In the higher echelons of this group are high school teachers, small businessmen, and minor civil servants.

Among the people who appear before the court there is often a "rich" brother or a "boss," but these terms are purely relative; seldom, if ever, does a really wealthy man appear.

Like all other American Jews, these people aspire to send their children to college. They often succeed, and the records of the court are full of parents who refer proudly to their son the doctor or the professor. But the educational ambitions of these people also fail much more often than they do among other American Jews. In these families there are more drop-outs, more bright children who can't afford to go to college, more sons who graduate from high school and get jobs driving a truck or operating a lathe.

Another characteristic of this community is its "foreignness." It is much closer in feeling, even in manners, to its European origins than most American Jewish communities. Back in 1937, in a newspaper column about the court, Ernie Pyle wrote that one-third of the litigants could speak only Yiddish. The percentage is certainly much lower today but still high enough so that at least one or two of the judges must know Yiddish for the court to function properly. Most of the cases nowadays are conducted in English, but frequently a litigant will break into Yiddish in the heat of emotion, or, groping for a specific, colorful, usually insulting expression, he will find that only a Yiddish one can do the job. High on Mrs. Richman's list of friendly inexpensive psychiatrists is one who speaks Yiddish.

At the same time the people who come to the court are very "American." Along with their attachment to the old ways, they have the immigrant's urgent desire to become part of the new. They are almost all patriots;

they want to make it clear to the whole world that they are Americans. Thus the president of the Polish Kossover Society—a group founded in 1914 and consisting of men in their sixties or over who came originally from the same town in Poland—proudly tells the court that they have just changed the name to "The Kossover Young Men of America." He is expressing, in simple form, an ambivalence that runs through a great many cases.

These people are closer than most other American Jews to the essence of their heritage. They may not be more religious—many are Orthodox, but many are also Conservative and Reform—but they have the attachment to Jewish manners, to the flavor of Jewish life, that characterized even the radical atheists among the early immigrants. When a judge admonishes a man for refusing to abide by the decision, he puts his indignation in these words: "What kind of a *Jew* are you to stand before this court and turn your back?"

In the old days these people had yet another trait in common; they mostly lived on the Lower East Side, within half a dozen miles of one another. Today they have dispersed all over the city. People come to the court from every borough. Despite this geographical diversity, however, the common bond of Jewishness still holds these people together and justifies us in calling them a community.

The relationship of the judges to this community is paradoxical. Most of the judges do not belong to it. They are successful men who move in social circles where clients of the court seldom are seen. Their level of education and of sophistication is usually superior to that of the people who appear before them. The rabbis who serve as judges tend to preside over synagogues that most of the litigants would never attempt to join. Occasionally there is a judge who actually lives and works in the same community as the litigants, but he will be somebody like the late Adolph Held, managing editor of *The Forward*, whose job gave him a special and exalted status.

At the same time, most of the judges came from this community originally, were born and brought up among the kind of people whose problems they are called upon to settle. While the circumstances of their lives are different now, their attitudes, assumptions, and values are fundamentally the same. This is crucial to their effectiveness.

The confidence they inspire is dependent, first of all, on each litigant feeling that he and the judges talk the same language. If the judges throw in a word or two of Yiddish from time to time, this is not because they fear the litigant won't understand their English but because they want him to accept them as one of his own kind. There is, for instance, a theatrical style that Jews love to indulge in, which they don't really expect anybody to take at face value.

A complaining husband: "When I am dead, I suppose I will have peace. But now I am living like somebody who is dead and who is being punished by God for his sins."

A complaining wife: "How long is a wife to be enslaved by a husband? Abraham Lincoln freed the slaves in 1865, but I am not to be freed ever!"

The judges indulge in the same kind of rhetoric when it suits them. Here is a judge addressing Mr. Schoenberg, who has been accused of turning his children against his estranged wife:

"I am saying this to you, Mr. Schoenberg, with all the vigor at my command and all the frankness I possess. It is the most outrageous thing in the world if you did, or if you do, or if you *should* do anything that would alienate the children's affections from their mother. It is the bum and loafer, the drunkard and the thief, the lowbrow and the scum of the earth who treats his wife in that kind of manner. I resent any man's acting towards a woman in this way, and a man acting that way towards his wife and the mother of his children is really low!" Having delivered himself of this tirade, the judge lowers his voice and goes on in his usual amiable tone, "Mind you, I am not charging you with this, as your wife does. I am telling you only that your conscience will have to be your guide." In cold print it may seem as if the judge has totally destroyed his rapport with Mr. Schoenberg. But this is not the case. They are both at home in the same rhetorical atmosphere; they understand each other perfectly.

This mutual understanding is necessary; the community sees the judges as guardians of its highest moral and social standards. The community is willing to put its trust in them because they are spokesmen for all those values that it most esteems. In the entire history of the court no litigant has ever objected to any of the judges. This is not because all of them do the job equally well; there *have* been inept ones. But in all of the Board's records I cannot find a single instance of a judge who has ever expressed an opinion or elucidated a principle (of any importance) that did not accord with the

opinions and principles of the community. This circumstance arises out of neither hypocrisy nor calculation
nor cowardice. The simple truth is that these men *are*
in accord with the community.

The community knows this perfectly well and ap-
preciates the value of having an august body to remind
it from time to time of its own standards. At the end of
the case of the Polish villagers who published unflattering material about their *landsmen* killed by the Nazis,
the complainant put into words what most members of
the community feel about the court. "You have made
right a great wrong," he said. "But more important,
these men *know* now that it is wrong. And that is the
main thing."

But the function of the judges is not merely to be
mirrors of community standards. Within limits—and
everybody *feels* what those limits are, though nobody
can define them specifically—the judges are also supposed to develop and improve the standards, to be leaders of the community.

Thirty years ago, for instance, the court used its
moral influence to bring an end to certain dubious but
traditional practices in the treatment of synagogue employees. Today the court is pushing hard, against much
community prejudice, for a more tolerant view of mental and emotional problems. It is trying to make its
clients understand that psychiatric treatment does not
shame the patient and to convince them that many
forms of aberrant behavior should be looked upon as
illnesses rather than crimes. These include alcoholism,
narcotics addiction, sexual promiscuity, even certain
kinds of violence, all of which were beyond the pale of
judges of a generation ago.

## Prestige

And so the paradoxical position of the judges—their being *from* the community but not *in* it—is necessary if they are to carry out their double function as leaders and reflectors. They live uptown, though they were born downtown. They move in lofty circles and serve on important boards and committees, though without ever forgetting their Yiddish. They are able to assume, along with all their homely down-to-earth qualities, an air of stern superiority. They have enough prestige and distance to impose change and progress on the community; at the same time their instinct and background lead them to accept the community's values and share its attitudes.

What are these values and attitudes? It is not my intention to provide an organized detailed analysis of them. They will emerge by themselves from the individual case histories that make up the rest of this book. The true nature of this community is delineated in the records of the court. Bursting forth from these records come judges and litigants, husbands and wives, doddering old parents and cocky children, sick men, madmen, confidence men, victims, fools, heroes, beasts of prey, would-be suicides, irrepressible optimists—a whole world of pathetic, hateful, charming, noble, and exasperating human beings. One thing they all have in common is the ability, in fact the compulsion, to open their mouths and reveal themselves.

# CHAPTER

# 6

❦ ❦
❦

## *Lovers*

In the community served by the Jewish Conciliation
Board real life is hardly considered to exist outside marriage. Boys and girls get married at a comparatively
early age. Men and women who have been divorced or
widowed usually marry a second time. There are very
few old maids or confirmed bachelors.

Much importance is attached, therefore, to the
preparations that lead up to marriage—the morality of
premarital sex, the selection of a proper mate, the ritual
of courtship, the wedding itself. In connection with
these important preliminaries disputes naturally arise,
and sometimes they end up in the court.

Let us begin with a form of preliminary that no
longer exists.

Mrs. Leona Glick is a matchmaker, one of the best
known on the Lower East Side. She belongs to an old

profession that, back in Europe, served a useful, even an essential, purpose. Because marriages were arranged by the young couple's parents, a knowledgeable and trustworthy intermediary, somebody with reliable information about the personal qualities of bride and groom and the financial and social positions of their families, was more than worth his fee. But when the matchmaker came to America along with his fellow immigrants, his position instantly became ambiguous. Those who made use of his services felt uneasily that he belonged to a dead past, that his presence on the American scene was somehow undignified, and this feeling was reflected in the slightly unscrupulous way they treated him. In the early days of the court Mrs. Glick and her professional colleagues often had to bring their clients up on charges.

The records of the court show that Mrs. Glick was involved in three cases between 1937 and 1945.

In the first case Mrs. Bosky, a middle-aged lady, much intimidated by all the people in the courtroom, starts telling her story in a low voice. "I want her to return my money to me—"

A judge interrupts. "What kind of money? Speak a little louder, won't you?"

Mrs. Bosky raises her voice slightly. "I was a widow many years. As long as I was with my children, life was full, and I never thought of getting married again. But children grow up, they leave as birds leave the nest. The house became empty, I was alone with myself day and night—I thought it would be a good idea to do something about it. I saw this matchmaker's name in the newspaper, so I went to her in her office. She asked for $25 in advance for introducing me to a husband. I gave her the money, and here is my receipt."

"Did she ever introduce you to a man?" the judge asks.

Mrs. Bosky's voice is loud and clear now. "I met him, but he was not my type. He was too young for me."

"That was the only man she introduced you to?"

"She introduced me to another. He was also not my type—he couldn't even speak English properly. And there were two or three more. A matchmaker only gets money if she finds something for you. She didn't find anything, so she should give me my money back."

The judges call on Mrs. Glick now, and she rises. She is a striking figure—of indeterminate age, overdressed, wearing too much makeup, with a bird's nest of orange hair that makes no hypocritical pretense at being her own. Nevertheless, nobody thinks of her as being low or vulgar. The chief impression she makes is one of overwhelming refinement and gentility. She looks (according to one court reporter of the thirties) "like a *grande dame* at the opera." She is known to speak Yiddish, as a matter of business, but clearly she prefers to speak English—which she does now, in pear-shaped, elocution-teacher tones.

"I feel that my business is a reliable one," she says, smiling confidently at the judges, looking not a bit uneasy or remorseful. "I have many letters from couples who, thanks to me, are enjoying very happy marriages. I don't make money for doing nothing. I told this lady that she must pay me $25, and more after that if I found a man who was good for her."

"I was ready to give her $100," Mrs. Bosky breaks in. "But if—"

"I did whatever I could for this lady," says Mrs. Glick. "After all, it is in my own interest to get people together, because I really make my money after people are married. But I don't know what else I can do for this lady. I introduced her to many men, and none of them appealed to her. She herself doesn't know what she wants. It's a common situation in my business. An individual wishes to get married, but when it comes to the point, he or she doesn't wish to get married to *somebody*."

"If she finds me so difficult to match up with somebody," says Mrs. Bosky, "why shouldn't she return the money to me?"

Mrs. Glick gives an indulgent little laugh. "Excuse me, but the money she paid me I will not be able to return. She must understand that this is not Europe where you carry your business from door to door, in your pocket. Here in America you do things in a modern way. I have an office, a reception room, a telephone. I must place advertisements in the newspaper. I have an overhead."

"She couldn't find a man for me," Mrs. Bosky insists. "Why should I pay for her overhead?"

But the judges recognize the justice of Mrs. Glick's position, and they decide that Mrs. Bosky is not entitled to her money back. They suggest, however, that Mrs. Glick make a few more attempts to find a man for Mrs. Bosky. "After all," says one of the judges, "something is always possible."

Three years later, in the second case involving Mrs. Glick, the complainant is completely different from Mrs. Bosky. Her name is Vera Brodie, and she is in her thirties, well-educated, highly Americanized. She has never been married. She is an executive in a small advertising agency; she is efficient, well-groomed, sophisticated. Until recently she lived with her mother, but last year her mother died. Shortly afterward it occurred to her that she would like to get married.

"I read an article in a magazine," she explains to the judges, "in which the author pointed out that marriages arranged by families or through marriage brokers have as much chance of success as any other type of marriage. After all, this author wrote, there is a moment in every relationship when the man and the woman are unknown to each other and meet, more or less accidently, for the first time. I was intrigued by the thought, and shortly afterward I happened to see Mrs. Glick's advertisement in *The Jewish Daily Forward*—my mother subscribed to it regularly, and the subscription still has a year or two to run. I visited Mrs. Glick at her office, and I was favorably impressed by her manner, and so I gave her a $25 deposit. That was well over ten months ago. She has succeeded in doing nothing for me. I feel that I am entitled to the return of my money."

In her defense Mrs. Glick again states that she introduced the client to a great many men, none of whom suited her.

"Every one of her selections was quite impossible," says Miss Brodie. "Yes, she told me that the deposit was nonreturnable, but this assumes some kind of efficient procedure on her part. If she were a good matchmaker, she should be a judge of human nature, she would have known that the people she introduced me to were not for me."

Mrs. Glick is not about to sit still for any aspersions on

her ability to judge human nature. "Unfortunately," she says, "I know this lady's type very well. She is the type that nobody is good enough for. She expects me to give her something on a golden platter. She doesn't understand that there are no magic tricks in this world. I'm sorry for her, but she must realize that I cannot give her the luck she lost years ago."

Once again the judges decide in Mrs. Glick's favor.

Mrs. Glick's third case is five years later, and this time she is the complainant. The defendant is a second cousin of hers, Louis Flaks, a paper-box manufacturer, fairly well-to-do. Unable to find a husband for his unmarried daughter, he went to Mrs. Glick for help. He paid her the usual $25 deposit and agreed to pay another $125 if she came up with the right man. "You understand," Mrs. Glick says, "this was much less than my usual fee. I was giving him a special rate because it was in the family."

It wasn't long before Mrs. Glick produced a young man, a refugee from the Nazis, whose qualifications were excellent. Flaks invited the young man for dinner at his house, and that was the last Mrs. Glick heard of the matter—until a few months later she learned through the family grapevine that the wedding had taken place four weeks earlier. She went to Flaks and asked for her $125, and he told her she would have to wait, so she has brought him to court.

The judge's first question to Flaks is "Why didn't you invite Mrs. Glick to the wedding?"

"There were many I didn't invite," Flaks says.

Mrs. Glick puts in, "You invited my nephew!"

"You don't deny you made this arrangement, do you,

Mr. Flaks?" the judge says. "So why won't you give Mrs. Glick $125?"

"I'll give her $25 now," Flaks says. "I'll give her the rest if my daughter and this fellow stay together. If they break up, why should I be out $100?"

The judges decide that Flaks should give Mrs. Glick $125 and this should not depend on whether or not the young couple stay together. "She's done her part of the job," the judges say. "When two young people marry, no one knows."

"I'd rather give it to charity," Flaks declares.

"Pay it to her in ten days," says the judge.

This case was heard in 1945. What became of Mrs. Glick afterward? The records of the court cannot tell us. She appears in no more cases, and neither, after a few years, do any other members of her profession.

Once the prospective bride and groom come together, with or without the help of a matchmaker, a variety of obstacles can arise to their getting married. The court's function, as conceived by the judges, is either to find some way of removing those obstacles or to persuade the interested parties to reconcile themselves to them.

Mr. and Mrs. Bellin live in Brooklyn, where he works as a plumber. Mrs. Bellin was born in America, but Mr. Bellin came from Poland after the war. They have a nineteen-year-old son and a seventeen-year-old daughter who is entering her last year of high school. As Mrs. Bellin puts it, "Seventeen is a rough age. My son went through it, and he is trying to simmer down now, but the girl is suddenly coming into this age. She uses the phone too much. She's always on the phone. And she met this boy who is twenty. She says she is in love with him. She is invited to affairs with his parents. He came here from Hungary three years ago, and he is not like American boys. He is not as aggressive. But my husband feels a child her age should not go out so much."

Mr. Bellin's accent is thick; combined with his agitation, this makes him hard to understand. "Last year, after so many years in this country," he says, "for the first time some people stopped me in the street and said that my daughter is with this boy too much. I put in a law that she has to be home by dark. Does she listen to me? Does she obey me? No! I am not interested in this boy or in a thousand boys. When *my* parents said something to me, that was it, even when I was more than seventeen!"

Mrs. Bellin disagrees with her husband. She says that her daughter, Susan, sees the boy only on weekends, that he always brings her home before midnight, that the boy means no harm but seems sincere in his desire to marry the girl someday. "My husband had a very hard life," Mrs. Bellin says. "He becomes so incensed that logic flies out the window."

Mr. Bellin shakes these words away. "This is nothing new to me," he says. "They think I know nothing. The children will decide for themselves. My opinion is overruled by the weaker sex."

The parents are sent out of the room, and Susan is called in. She has a string of complaints about her father: he's never satisfied; he yells at her for saying things she never said; if she's happy, he gets jealous; if she's sad, he reprimands her for not being happy; everything she does is no good. Then she talks about Billy, her boyfriend—how intelligent he is, how kind and gentle he is, how hard he works, how much they want to get married after she finishes school. The judges lecture her on being tolerant and obedient to her father. "He has certain values and standards," one judge says. "He thinks that if his children live this way too, they will be nicer people. He loves you very much, but also he has a great deal of pride."

Her answer is "He wants me to go in his Polish ways. I can't. I'm an American."

The rabbi says, "Many parents have ideas of restricting children under eighteen. I don't know how Polish this idea is." But clearly the judges are on the side of American young love. Their "decision" is really a long lecture to Mr. Bellin on giving children a chance to live their own lives. "What you have to do is say to yourself, 'I can't hold the line as strong as I hold it. Each has to give up something.' "

This lecture has its effect on the outraged father, though there is nothing conciliatory about his way of showing it. "All right, let her go with him, let her do what she wants with him! Only don't let me know about it! After they're married you can tell me, but until then I don't want to know a thing!"

Mrs. Samuelson is a widow with an only child, a daughter who is going to college. Mrs. Samuelson's brother, Albert Lesser, has been like a father to this girl ever since her real father died. These people are American born, college educated, as different from the Bellins as they could be. Their case takes place within the last three years.

Mrs. Samuelson has subjected her daughter Lorna to none of the old-fashioned old-country strictness. The girl has been going out on dates since she was fifteen; she has been encouraged to choose her own friends, have her own ideas, and live her own life. She has been allowed to understand that, when the time came, she would naturally choose her own husband. The time has now come; from her college town in Connecticut, Lorna has brought home Neil Engel and announced that she wants to marry him. Mrs. Samuelson is terribly upset, and she wants the court to force Lorna to break up the affair. Lorna's uncle Albert joins in on this request.

What have they got against the boy? "He is the most unrespectable person she could choose for a friend," says Mrs. Samuelson. "He makes her drink. It's a pity a young girl like that should drink. I am afraid of him. He may cause an accident. I want to protect my daughter from him."

Neil and Lorna step forward, and the story of Neil's "drinking" is explained. The truth is, he hardly ever drinks. But once, when he was upset over the death of a close friend, he had a drink before he came to take Lorna out, and her mother has been making an issue out of this ever since. As for the charge that he makes Lorna drunk, this is equally ridiculous. Lorna has an eye condition. She is allergic to pollen in the air, and her eyes grow red very easily. Her mother knows this perfectly well, but insists on attributing the redness to drinking.

Under questioning the real reason emerges for Mrs. Samuelson's objection to Neil. He comes from a refugee family. He himself wasn't born in this country but was brought here as a small child. His parents have less money that Mrs. Samuelson and her brother. He has to work his way through college, and his grades are lower than Lorna's. Uncle Albert says to the judges, "We wanted to see this girl grow up a 'one and only,' as people predicted. It was obvious she would be superior in everything, way above average. She was so bright in school, always skipping classes. Last night I tried to reason with her, saying, 'Can't you pick a boy that is more on your level? All our work and all our efforts are only for you. Can't you give us this one privilege of picking a higher-type boy?' Years from now I am sure she will be thankful to us if we persuade her to get rid of this boy."

The judges spend a lot of time talking with Lorna and Neil, trying to determine how they feel about each other. They are especially concerned about the seriousness of Neil's intentions. He swears that he intends to marry Lorna as soon as he gets out of college. They ask him why he has made no move to establish good relations with Lorna's mother. He says that he has: "I used to wear dungarees but now I wear conservative clothes. My hair used to be long but I cut it. I did these things to try to please Mrs. Samuelson."

The judges end up accepting the basic view of Lorna's mother and uncle—the girl could do better than Neil Engel. They suggest that Lorna should go to a psychotherapist in the hope of improving her self-image. But the judges are realists, so they also tell Mrs. Samuelson that she must not try to keep Lorna from seeing Neil, she must not talk against the boy, and if the relationship ends in marriage, she must accept that as cheerfully as possible. The boy may not be any Prince Charming, but he *is* hard-working and respectable and Jewish. A girl could do worse.

*74*

## Lovers

Marriage is such a blessed state that the judges will recommend it for practically everybody under almost any circumstances. But there are exceptions. Sometimes one party or the other is so repulsive that even the judges can't stomach him.

Chaim Zulnitz came from Poland when he was seventeen and has been in America nine years. Joan Goodovitch was born in America and works as a secretary. A few months ago they became engaged, and he bought her a coat, a bracelet, and a $200 diamond ring. Last month she broke off the engagement, so he has brought her to court. He wants her either to marry him, as she agreed, or to give him back his gifts.

"Why did she break the engagement?" the judge asks.

"Who knows why?" Zulnitz says. "I asked her a little favor, and she got mad and said she was through with me."

"A little favor!" Joan cries. "He asked me to sign a paper before the rabbi that if I ever decided to get a divorce from him I wouldn't demand alimony!"

The judge turns to Zulnitz. "You asked her to sign this paper?"

"Why not?" he says. "I'm not a rich man. If I wanted to get married a second time, I couldn't afford it with alimony on my back."

"Don't you think," says the judge, "that it's a little unusual to worry about alimony before the wedding?"

"What's unusual? I know what goes on here in America with this. I have read all about it in the newspapers. What I asked from her was a simple thing that any girl who cared for me would be happy to do."

The judges decide that the girl doesn't have to marry

him. She does have to return his ring and his gifts, however. They congratulate her on her good fortune.

Another exception to the judges' rule: despite their commitment to the institution of marriage, they will not impose it on anybody against his will or attempt to intimidate anybody for backing out at the last minute. The shotgun wedding is definitely not part of the mores of this community.

Irwin Bross, twenty-six years old, a shipping clerk, is brought to court by Felicia Blumberg and her mother. Felicia has had an illegitimate baby, and she accuses Irwin of being the father.

The year is 1956. In 1940, when a similar case appeared before the court, there were cries of astonishment from the spectators, and the reporter from *The Forward* expressed the general feeling: "Who could believe that such a case was actually appearing before a *Jewish* court?" But today, as Felicia Blumberg comes out with her charges, nobody in the room bats an eyelash.

"What do you want from us?" asks a judge. "Do you want this man to support the child?"

"He's already giving me support," says Felicia. "I want him to marry me."

"Did he ever actually promise he would marry you?"

Felicia's mother can't keep quiet when she hears this question. "I should have so many good years all the times he made my daughter that promise!"

The judges turn to Irwin, who stands by grinning. "So how about it? You don't deny you fathered this child on Felicia here?"

"Who's denying?" Irwin says.

"All right then, why don't you marry her?"

"I won't. I don't love her."

"You loved her once, didn't you?"

"Never. Not even slightly."

The judges are stymied. Even if the arbitration agreement made it legally possible, no man should be forced into marriage against his will. The rabbi tries one last time. "Come on," he says with his friendliest smile, "take her out, get to know her. You might find out she is a nice girl."

This argument makes no impression on Irwin. The case is dismissed.

An old man appears before the court with a long white beard, a yamalke on his head, and *paes*, the long ear curls that denote piety among the extreme Orthodox. The spectators think he must be a rabbi having trouble with his congregation, and this seems to be confirmed when his name is called out, "Rabbi Joseph Farkas."

Then comes the complainant who is bringing charges against Rabbi Farkas. She is a lady in her early fifties, and her eyes are red from weeping. She is introduced to the judges as Mrs. Muller.

"I am a widow for ten years," she says. "This man, this rabbi, he went about with me all last summer, and he promised to marry me, and now he refuses to keep his promise."

"Why?" one of the judges asks.

"I don't know. Months he went with me. He took me everywhere. He even took me to see the house he was going to buy for us to live in. He always talked to me so nicely. He said, 'This is all for you, all for you, my dearest.' And he always promised me the joys of life. I was planning to go with him to buy the furniture."

"What furniture? For what?"

"For the home he promised me—for our little nest! I kept telling him, the time is getting short, we ought to set the date. And he said, 'As soon as we get the furniture.'"

By this time most defendants would have interrupted the complainant at least once. The judges instinctively glance at Rabbi Farkas, waiting for some indignant protest to burst out of him. But the rabbi just stands there without looking at Mrs. Muller or showing by the smallest twitch of an eyebrow that he is the least bit perturbed at her accusations. On his face is a thoughtful smile, and his hands are clasped in front of him. He appears to be in a state of pious meditation. When it becomes clear that he has no intention of saying anything, the judges turn back to Mrs. Muller.

"So did you ever set the date? When did he tell you he'd marry you?"

"He never said when. He kept putting it off."

"Well, then, what do you want from us?"

"I want either he should marry me or he should give me some compensation."

"Compensation for what? Did he take any money from you?"

"He would have taken money from me if I would have given it to him."

"If he didn't take money from you, you have nothing legal against him."

"He made a fool of me," Mrs. Muller cries. "I'm not just an ordinary woman. My late husband was a well-known personality. I was always respected by my friends and neighbors. And now he has made my name ugly. I am ashamed to walk out on the street."

"People will forget," says the rabbi-judge in his kindly tone. "Wouldn't you be happier if you did the same?"

"I can't forget. What he did to me—is that how a rabbi acts? Is that nice?"

"Coming to court, bringing such charges," says the businessman-judge, "is *that* nice?"

But Mrs. Muller is too excited to notice the rebuke. "You can't do such things to people! Now he has ten other women with whom he is doing the same thing. We should not allow such things to go on. We must make an end of such behavior. A man with a beard doesn't act this way!"

A certain amount of suppressed laughter is heard from the spectators.

"Mrs. Muller, what can we do?" says the rabbi-judge. "We can't make this man marry you against his will, and there is no law that gives money for breach of promise. If Rabbi Farkas wishes to say anything to explain or excuse his actions—"

Again the judges look at Rabbi Farkas expectantly. He looks up at them for a moment, gives a modest, deprecating smile, and lowers his eyes, returning to his meditations.

This infuriates the spectators. Cries are heard: "We want to hear him!" "He should have a chance to speak for himself!"

"Nobody has to speak if they don't want to," says the lawyer-judge. "If the charges themselves have no legal substance, he doesn't have to defend himself against them. The case is dismissed."

Amid the groans from the spectators a young man rises to his feet and addresses the judges angrily. "Allow me to say a few words. I am this woman's son-in-law. Such a man must be penalized and made to look a fool. After all, she is not the only one—"

"The law can't be changed," says the judge. "Case dismissed."

Mrs. Muller collapses weeping into her son-in-law's arms, and he leads her out of the court. Rabbi Farkas looks up at the judges with his soft smile, gives a little nod of thanks, and quietly leaves.

Finally the obstacles are cleared away, and the marriage can take place. The happy couple spend their last days of single life building up to the grand finale of the wedding. A wedding is a joyous affair, with lots of eating and drinking, dancing and making toasts, friends and relations from all over joining together in celebration. How could this joyous event possibly lead to a session in the Jewish court? But, of course, it isn't difficult. The very things that make the wedding such a festive occasion are fraught with potential dangers. Food and drink cost money. Guest lists are social dynamite. Everybody is in the kind of intense emotional state that aggravates old feuds and creates new ones.

A quiet man in his fifties brings an angry, red-faced man of about the same age up on charges. The quiet man introduces himself as Rabbi Perlberg. He says that he performed a wedding for the defendant's daughter; he claims that the defendant, Mr. Tannenbaum, still owes him $50.

The rabbi-judge breaks in. "Excuse me, I'm not quite clear. You married the girl in your synagogue?"

"I don't have a synagogue," says Rabbi Perlberg. "The ceremony took place in my small hall where we usually make parties and Jewish affairs."

"You mean to say you are a caterer also?"

"Exactly. In my small hall we put up a hoopah, and I perform the ceremony, and then we bring out meals and whiskey for the guests."

"What kind of meal?" The rabbi-judge seems both fascinated and repelled by the details of his fellow clergyman's business.

"Not a cooked meal, but cold cuts. It is more than enough. Everyone leaves happy. I only get a small profit, and there hasn't yet been a person who left my table hungry. After the Tannenbaum wedding, the bride and groom thanked me heartily, and they even gave my wife, who waits on the tables, a $5.00 tip."

The rabbi-judge can hardly contain his amazement. "The rebbitzin waits on tables and gets tips!"

At this point the defendant Tannenbaum is unable to keep quiet any longer. "So you heard him—his wife got $5.00 extra! So why does he come here now? We didn't pay him enough money already?"

"I don't say that people owe me money for no good reason," says Rabbi Perlberg. "I only ask what's coming to me. I have always had full faith in the people I deal with, and this is the first person who ever tried to do me out of anything. Believe me, it's not pleasant, with the New Year coming in a few days, to have an argument with a Jewish man. That's why I came here to this court instead of the regular court."

"At the wedding I paid everything to him!" Tannenbaum shouts. "After the wedding he suddenly decides he didn't get enough!"

Rabbi Perlberg keeps his temper and patiently explains his case. "I asked him for $2.50 for each person, for cold cuts. He agreed to this and said there would be sixty people. But at the wedding twenty more people came. I counted them myself—I counted eighty guests in all. I told him this before the party was over. I pointed out to him that he must pay for the extra guests. He was busy, so he said he'd pay me later. Now he won't pay me."

"If he spoke to me about this, I didn't hear," Tannenbaum says. "I shook hands with him at the door when I left, and he seemed satisfied. Not a word about eighty guests or $50."

"Because he told me already that he would pay me later. Was I supposed to keep reminding him? Naturally I expected a check in a day or two. A person who marries a daughter and tries to smuggle in extra guests for nothing is beyond me."

This statement infuriates Tannenbaum. He cries out that he always pays his debts, that he has a reputation for being an honest businessman, that he has never in his whole life been a cheapskate about money, especially where his children are concerned. It is clear that the money itself doesn't bother Tannenbaum nearly as much as being caught in such a shabby trick.

"Mr. Tannenbaum," says the rabbi-judge, "do you deny what this gentleman says, that extra people came to the wedding party?"

"I don't deny, I don't agree. I only know I invited only sixty. It might be that some people sneaked in just to eat. Was that my fault? It was his hall, he should have had a watchman on the door."

"The people who came were all known to him," says

Rabbi Perlberg. "There was nobody there who didn't talk to him. Some of the extra ones were sitting at his table, like members of his family."

"Mr. Tannenbaum," says the rabbi-judge in his most conciliatory voice, "it's a blessing when a daughter gets married to a nice young man. Even if there's a misunderstanding here, should you be picayune about a few dollars for your daughter's wedding?"

"By me it's the principle!" Tannenbaum says. "I don't owe anybody anything, and I won't pay anybody anything!" He turns on his heel and starts to walk out of the court.

The businessman-judge calls after him in a voice that has no conciliation in it at all. "You're in court, Mr. Tannenbaum! You must show respect! You don't leave till we've given our decision!"

Muttering under his breath, Tannenbaum returns to the bench.

The judges confer in low voices; this takes them only a minute or two. Then they inform Tannenbaum that he has to pay $50 to Rabbi Perlberg.

"It's not coming to him!" Tannenbaum cries. "I won't throw money out just like that!"

"You signed the agreement, and you'll stick by it," says the lawyer-judge sharply.

Tannenbaum does some more muttering, but finally he pulls out his checkbook.

The rabbi-judge beams on him and says, "You won't regret this, Mr. Tannenbaum. Think of the children, starting out in life together, with love and happiness in their hearts. Think of marriage and what a beautiful state it is. With such thoughts how can you go away angry?"

# CHAPTER

# 7

❦ ❦
❦

# *Husbands and Wives—One*

Half the cases that come to the court are disputes between husbands and wives. Marriage, as the rabbi says, may be a beautiful state of love and happiness, but when you spend hour after hour reading through the records of the Jewish Conciliation Board, it is hard to keep yourself from thinking that marriage for most people is a form of hell. Logically, of course, you know that this conclusion in untenable. Unhappy marriages are precisely what this court is supposed to deal with. Happy couples, who no doubt form the great majority, seldom have any reason to be here. Then you return to the records, to the steady outpouring of misery, desperation, and despair, and so much for logic.

Most shocking of all are the hatred and the bitterness that so many of these marriages distill. Sometimes these feelings are expressed in the comparatively harmless form of verbal invective. Certain epithets are popular through the years. In the twenties no less than in the sixties, a husband who really wants to draw blood will call his wife "prostitute," and she in turn will call him "bum." Also in favor is the horrendous insult that can be applied equally to both sexes—"anti-Semite." And many individuals seem to relish inventing new and original insults. A wife says to her husband, "How come that you live and other people are dying?" A husband says to his wife when she asks him what he wants from her, "It would only take five minutes for you to commit suicide!"

This verbal mud doesn't stick very long. Other kinds are much harder to wash off and are meant to be. It is extraordinary how ingenious married couples can be at finding ways to torment each other.

Mr. and Mrs. Rosen own two small houses in the Bronx. They and their children live in the first one; they rent out rooms in the second one. Mr. Rosen, an upholsterer, has just lost his job, and Mrs. Rosen is furious with him. "Every job he ever had he's lost," she says. "Every business he ever took up went bankrupt. He's destroyed everything he ever touched." In her anger she has thrown him out of the house. He has moved into an unrented room in the second house, and he is keeping himself alive by collecting the rent from the other tenants, because Mrs. Rosen has the bankbook for the joint savings account in her possession.

His struggle for survival, minimal though it is, has further inflamed Mrs. Rosen's anger. So now she has gone to the second house and turned off the heat and the water in Mr. Rosen's room. And she has told the tenants there that she will reduce their rents if they pay the money directly to her. Mr. Rosen comes to the court complaining that his wife is forcing him to sleep in the street. He arouses no pity in Mrs. Rosen. "Let him be a man," she says, "and I'll give him a place to sleep."

The judges decide that one house should be put entirely in Mr. Rosen's name and the other house entirely in Mrs. Rosen's name and that each shoud run his or her house without interference. This solves the immediate practical problem, but all efforts to calm Mrs. Rosen's fury are doomed to failure. She hates her husband much too intensely. She leaves the court complaining bitterly because the judges kept him from sleeping in the street.

Mr. and Mrs. Aaronson had an only child, Leonard, who died of spinal meningitis at the age of twenty. The grief-stricken parents bought a pair of cemetery plots next to his so that eventually they could all be buried together. On the headstone of Leonard's plot they had these words engraved: "When we die, we will live in love with our beloved son."

That was three years ago. The death of their son has slowly destroyed their marriage; he turned out to be the strongest bond between them. In the course of these three years they have grown increasingly bitter against each other and have engaged in increasingly malicious acts against each other. Finally, in a fit of pique against his wife, Mr. Aaronson has sold her cemetery plot next to their dead son's. She brings him to court to get the plot back. He justifies what he did on the grounds that she never felt enough grief over the boy's death, that the tragedy didn't crush her as it did him—which proves that she didn't really love the boy, so why should she be allowed to lie next to him?

The judges have no trouble coming to a decision. Obviously Mr. Aaronson must buy back his wife's plot no matter how much it costs him. But what judge can head off the next act of pointless cruelty that one or the other of these people will commit?

Mr. and Mrs. Karp are both in their seventies and have been married fifty years. She claims that they never got along, that she stayed with him only because of the children, that he always yells at her. Now that the children are grown up and married, she has found a unique way of expressing her hatred of her husband, and this is why he brings her to court.

"I belong to a burial society for eighteen years," says Mr. Karp. "I went in with her approval. I paid for her and for me. We got two nice graves next to each other in Staten Island. Now all of a sudden she says she won't be buried in the grave I bought for her. She went out and found her own grave, in a cemetery on Long Island. Why should it be that way? All right, I yelled at times. It is because I was hurt. When one is hurt, one yells. But why does this mean we shouldn't be buried together? Not to mention that I already paid the society for her grave and I couldn't get my money back."

The judges ask Mrs. Karp to tell her side of the story. She brings it all out in an angry, tearful rush. "To be married for fifty years to a man and not want to be buried in the same cemetery, don't you think there must be a good reason? He is a big person in his organizations and they think highly of him, but he is not that way at home, believe me. Because of how he is at home

I do not want to be in the same cemetery with him. I want to be separated from him when I am dead. I therefore will buy my own grave."

The judges now try to reason with her. "You are married for fifty years. After one hundred twenty years, when you leave this world, why are you afraid to be buried with him? You will be in your place, he will be in his place."

"I don't understand," says Mrs. Karp.

"Every person rests in his grave," says the rabbi. "Take my word for it, he won't bother you when you are dead."

But Mrs. Karp can't accept this idea. "I have been a slave for him," she says. "I therefore don't want to be in the same cemetery with him."

"Don't you think the children will suffer from this?" the rabbi asks. "It's a shame for the children that you should be separated. They will have to go to two separate cemeteries."

"My children are in Long Island. They both have cars, and in one-quarter of an hour they will be near my grave. To Staten Island they won't go nearly as much." And there is no mistaking the glitter of satisfaction in her eyes.

"Your children will also have children," says the rabbi. "The grandchildren will ask why they go to two separate cemeteries."

"My children will answer them. They know how I have lived."

The businessman-judge tries a different approach now. "Mrs. Karp, what will be if your husband lives longer than you and he will not bury you where you want—what will you do?"

"I thought of that," she answers. "I will make a will, and if he doesn't bury me there, I will request my children to call a policeman and make him bury me where I want to be buried."

In their decision the judges take note of the fact that Mr. Karp bought the grave eighteen years ago and cannot get his money back, while Mrs. Karp still hasn't closed the deal on the new grave. They also point out that Mr. Karp bought the grave with Mrs. Karp's full knowledge and permission. Therefore she has a financial as well as a marital obligation; she must agree to be buried next to her husband.

Mrs. Karp is unhappy with the decision, though the rabbi promises her again that once they are settled in their graves, her husband's yelling will stop.

Mr. Greenbloom gets angry at his wife after a fight and decides he must hurt her somehow. They both belong to a burial society and pay dues that entitle them to death endowments and funeral expenses. The secretary of the society, Katzman, is a crony of Greenbloom's so Greenbloom arranges for Katzman to send Mrs. Greenbloom a letter telling her that she is being expelled, that she can stop paying dues, and that she will lose all her benefits. Greenbloom doesn't mean this to be a real expulsion; it is his idea of a joke, just to give his wife aggravation. But the letter gives her so much aggravation that she gets a heart attack and dies.

Greenbloom now asks the society for his wife's funeral expenses and the death endowment. The society, at Katzman's suggestion, takes the position that Greenbloom, in requesting that letter of expulsion, was in effect withdrawing his wife from membership. The society, therefore, doesn't owe him a penny.

Greenbloom pleads with Katzman, "But you know it was only a joke!"

Katzman looks him straight in the eye and says, "Who's going to believe that any sane man would make such a joke on his own wife?"

The judges upheld Katzman's contention.

There is a real mystery here. How can we account for all this nastiness, vindictiveness, sometimes even out-and-out violence among members of a community who, by tradition and training and habit, tend to be essentially peace-loving? Maybe this is something that happens to people when they get married. Maybe the closeness of the relationship intensifies traits that were already there, making virtues noble but also making faults and weaknesses malignant.

This seems to be the view of Dr. Samuel Weiss, a psychiatrist who often sees patients referred by the court. In his report on one of the cases he writes, "From my experience it is my feeling that there is often a sadistic-masochistic spouse relationship in the typical Jewish Conciliation Board marital case, with the husband and the wife assuming either role in a consistent fashion." He goes on, in reference to the specific case he is writing about, to point out the dependence of the couple on the very pattern of violence, anger, and rejection that has brought them into court. He concludes that nothing can be done for them because the weaknesses in the character of each find their counterparts in the weaknesses of the other. They need the conflicts of their marriage as desperately as hungry people need food.

The same point is made many times by other psychiatrists with whom the Board consults. And there are many cases in which even a layman can observe the mechanism in operation.

Mr. and Mrs. Greenberg come to court for the third time in the last six years. They are both in their forties, and they have two children. Mrs. Greenberg, a large and formidable-looking woman, accuses her husband of beating her, the same charge she made on each of her previous appearances. Mr. Greenberg is a head shorter than she, probably weighs ten pounds less, and has a good-natured manner. Yet he admits the charge against him.

"It's really true that you beat her?" says the judge, measuring the two of them with his eyes.

"Yes, it's true," Greenberg says.

"Is that right, Mr. Greenberg? Is that proper?"

"No, it isn't right."

"Then why do you beat her?"

Greenberg looks guilty and confused. "What choice does she give me?" he says. "It's the only way of dealing with her. She nags and nags, and the house is miserable, and only when I beat her will she become quiet for a while."

Later the judges ask Mrs. Greenberg, "Why do you let him beat you?"

"How can I stop him?" she says. "That's why I come here to court. I'm asking you to stop him."

The judges dutifully deliver the same lecture to Greenberg that they have delivered in the past—how indecent and immoral it is for a husband to use violence against his wife. But the irrelevance of this lecture is probably obvious to everybody. In some obscure way Mr. and Mrs. Greenberg can only be satisfied when she has a grievance against him and he feels guilty toward her. They are, in the grimmest possible sense, made for each other.

If the cause of the marital dispute isn't rooted unchangeably in the characters of husband and wife, then it is rooted just as unchangeably in their social conditions—a view that is held by various observers of the court. "The wife's charges," wrote a reporter for *The Forward,* "are often merely excuses. She tries to pin things on him because she has so many troubles of her own that can't be cured—she has too little money, she's growing older, her children are moving away. She imagines he feels better about life than she does, so she makes him the scapegoat. He, in turn, knows he has plenty of troubles, and so her accusations irritate him and he answers them sharply. Soon they are fighting every day, and neither one of them knows what the fight is all about. The fight is not about themselves but about their poverty, cramped quarters, ill health, dull work—in short, the world they live in. But this they cannot see, and if they did, they could not bear to face it. They would rather hide from this terrible truth by playing the role of enemies."

Once again there are many cases that seem to bear out this analysis. Since the war the court has frequently handled a special version of this kind of marital dispute. Here is Mr. Linowitz, a Polish refugee who spent the war in a concentration camp, talking about his second marriage: "I had a former wife who was burnt. I had a son and daughter who were also burnt. When I came to America, I weighed sixty pounds after being in the concentration camp. The doctor told me, 'You are sick and even in ten years you won't be better. Look for a woman who will put you on your feet, get a wife who will be a companion.' I married this woman when I was paralyzed on one side. If I didn't get crazy from the concentration camp, I am made of iron. She too had been in a concentration camp, and I thought she would understand because she had plenty of tragedy. But all she does is twist what I say and torture me. I have sugar sickness, diabetes, and she says, 'Get burnt from your sugar.'"

It almost doesn't matter what Mr. and Mrs. Linowitz may be like "characterologically." Their marriage is doomed not by who they are but by what the world has done to them. No amount of advice, even if it comes from the wisest judges in the world, will ever free them from the concentration camp.

A fairly common view, then, about the marital problems that appear before the court is that most of them are hopeless; their psychological and social causes make them incurable.

By and large, however, this is not the view held by the court or its judges. They make no Pollyanna-like claim that they can settle everything with a kindly speech, but they also reject the totally pessimistic assertion that they can do nothing. They are too realistic for the first extreme and too idealistic for the second. Their attitude might be described as reluctant optimism.

This attitude is grounded, first of all, in the oldest,

most sacred Jewish values. The cornerstone of the good life, according to Jewish law, is marriage and the family. Commandments, injunctions, prayers, holidays—almost all are peculiarly oriented to protect the family. Jewish law recognizes that family life often involves inner conflict, tension, even misery, but regardless of these things, it must be kept together. The judges, whenever they are confronted by a marital problem, start off with the assumption that it *can* be solved because Torah and Talmud declare that it *must* be solved. Rarely will the judges recommend divorce for a couple, no matter how bitter and nasty their marriage seems to be.

This religious conviction is accompanied by a psychological theory. Once a man and woman get married, the judges seem to believe, this very fact creates an undying bond between them. No matter how bad the marriage may appear to be on the surface, no matter how hostile or incompatible the two parties, somewhere down deep they love each other. This does not mean that divorce can never be allowed; sometimes the bond of love has been driven so deep that it is unable to rise to the surface again. Nevertheless, love is there, and part of the judges' job is to try and make the hostile parties aware of it.

It is easy to laugh at this sanguine view of marriage. Plenty of times during the court sessions the application of this view produces comic effects. Mr. and Mrs. Wallach have been hurling charges at each other ever since they got to court. Now it is time for the judges to render a decision. "My dear people," says the rabbi in his most mellifluous voice, "listen now to the advice of the judges, and you will find it good. Two people who have lived together for so long must regain peace and harmony in their marriage—" As the rabbi purrs on, Mr. and Mrs. Wallach, standing next to each other, continue to bicker in low voices. "How dare you say that you never struck me?" "It is not so, when did I strike you?" "You struck me that time when we were at your mother's seder." "I never struck you! My hand slipped by accident!" "Oh, yes, I know you and your accidents!" Meanwhile, apparently oblivious of any of this, the rabbi moves into an inspiring peroration: "Be good to each other, consider each other's feelings, recognize the love you have for each other, and you will discover *sholom bais,* the crown and glory of a contented life—"

It is also easy to point out cynically that the judges themselves, with their increasing emphasis on the value of psychiatric treatment, are admitting by implication the inadequacy of the old traditional attitude toward marriage. In the first thirty years of the Board's existence, the judges seemed to feel that marital disputes could be settled through specific compromises or clear-cut pragmatic advice. The husband was advised to buy his wife a new coat or to stop yelling at the children; the wife was advised to cook better meals or to spend more time at the hairdresser. The implication was that as soon as a few simple remedies were applied, the natural love between husband and wife would start flowing again. In 1954 the Board's files include the first reference to marriage counseling: a disgruntled couple, instead of being shunted off with some benevolent words about going out together to a restaurant and a show, are referred to the Alfred Adler Consultation Service. Today, whatever else it may involve, nearly every decision in a marital case involves the recommendation that the parties should go to a marriage counselor or a psychiatrist. Despite their faith in the powers of love, the judges seem to have decided that some problems won't be solved by nature plus a little common sense; they have to be taken to professionals.

And so we smile indulgently at the rabbi-judge who quotes an old Jewish saying to an angry couple: "When a husband and wife keep on quarreling and fighting with each other, there is a storm in heaven." Very nice, but since when can you stop a storm with an adage?

And yet things happen in court that make us wonder.

A wife comes out with a long list of incredibly outrageous, cruel, and unreasonable things her husband has done to her throughout the twenty-five years of their marriage. "Why do you live with him?" asks one of the judges. And the wife replies in astonishment, "What do you mean? We're married, aren't we?"

A husband who has come to court to charge his wife with the most dreadful crimes begins his harangue in this way: "I want that woman. I want to live with her. She made me plenty of trouble. She made me lose my first wife, a respectable woman. She gave me so much that I fell for her, and I love her now. She came to me with her daughter who is twelve years old. That girl is the worst kid the world created. I hate that woman for what she makes me go through with her daughter. I won't leave that woman ever!"

A husband and wife stand in front of the judges for half an hour saying wounding, vicious things to each other. At one point the husband pulls out a handkerchief to wipe his eyes because he is crying. A little later his wife starts crying, so he passes the handkerchief over to her. She says, "Thank you," blows her nose in the handkerchief, hands it back to him, and then starts insulting him again.

In actions as well as words the court's old-fashioned view of marriage often seems to be confirmed. The fact is, bitterly hostile couples do go away reconciled to each other. The reconciliation probably doesn't end the pain and the conflict; their hour in court doesn't suddenly make their marriages idyllic; but somehow or other they seem to find a way of going on. It is significant that one particular kind of strategy has been used successfully by the judges through the years. Mrs. Gold's case is typical. She insists that she must get a divorce immediately; life with her husband would be intolerable for another day. The judges order a month's separation instead. Then she is to return to court and ask for her divorce again. At the end of the month she returns and says that she doesn't want the divorce anymore. "I have never felt so alone as all these weeks. All right, he has his faults. But I need him."

Maybe the psychiatrists and the sociologists are right. Maybe Mrs. Gold's "need" is just another word for inescapable social conditions or "a sadistic-masochistic spouse relationship." The court prefers to see it as love, grounded in a sense of duty toward the Jewish family. This may be a delusion, but without it the court probably could not function.

# CHAPTER

# 8

# Husbands and Wives—Two

Obviously the judges of the court would like to be able to attack and eliminate the fundamental causes of marital problems that come before them. But these are no easier to recognize than the fundamental causes of anything else. Most of the time the judges must be content with attacking the superficial causes—the things people *say* they are quarreling about, the reasons they give to others and to themselves. The court's working theory seems to be that if you hammer away hard enough at these surface complaints, you may just happen to hit against something deeper. A critic of the court might contend that this is a little bit like trying to cure leprosy with applications of cold cream, but the judges would probably answer, "Have you got any better suggestions? So what can it hurt to try?"

By far the most common subject for arguments between these husbands and wives is money. This is hardly surprising in a community where even the richest people are living pretty close to the bone. There are dozens of marital cases every year in which the wife accuses the husband of being unable to earn a decent living, the husband accuses the wife of squandering what he earns, one party discovers (usually by stumbling on a carelessly hidden bankbook) that the other party has been salting away money in a secret account. In many of these cases it is hard to know whether or not the problem goes any deeper than scarcity of money. If the couple could afford to get a bigger apartment, move to a better neighborhood, fix the kids' teeth, hire a cleaning woman, wouldn't everything be all right between them?

Take the phenomenon of stinginess, which is common in this community. The records of the court are crowded with misers whose convoluted efforts to keep from spending money are worthy of Molière or Gogol. "If I ask him for money," Mrs. Kleinman complains about her husband, "he tells me fifty years from now I won't need it. I was five dollars short one week, and I got the mail and noticed he was getting a check for $711 from the New York Life Insurance. Dividends, as the policies have been all paid up. I had to resort to being a detective. Of course, I didn't open the envelope, but through the light I could see the amount, $711. When I asked him for the five dollars, he said he doesn't have any money. So I told him here is a check, and he pushed me and said, 'This check will be for your funeral expense.' "

Can the Kleinmans of this world be explained simply

as pathological cases, or would their stinginess disappear if their incomes were doubled? There is evidence to support both views. It is clear, for instance, even from what their complaining wives say about them, that many of these misers are stingy not because they love money in itself but because of the anxiety that poverty grinds into them every day. "This man has a disease working for a rainy day," says one wife. "Do we know when the rainy day is? But when I ask him for an extra dollar, it has to be put away for a rainy day." And another wife says, "He doesn't drink or gamble or run around with women. But all his money he puts in a bank, saying the children should have it when he dies. I say to him, you are not living the right way *now*. I need the money *now*, I can't feed the family on crackers."

On the other hand, it is equally clear that many of these misers are well enough fixed so that they don't have to grasp at every penny. Poverty in their early years may have made them stingy, but today, for these men, poverty is a state of mind rather than an actual condition. The case of Jack Plissner is typical. Once poor, now comparatively rich, he enjoys the pleasures of conspicuous consumption. He buys fur coats and expensive jewelry for his wife, but she has to bring him to court in order to get enough money for her weekly household expenses. The judge says to Plissner, "An empty stomach under a Persian lamb is not understandable."

Miserliness tends to be highly resistant to persuasion. It can hardly ever be conciliated away. Faced with a hard case, the judges are often forced to take hard measures.

Mr. and Mrs. Lubin are in their late fifties, with a married daughter and a son who goes to college and lives with them. Mr. Lubin works as a tailor for one of the big department stores, and while he is far from being wealthy, he makes a nice living.

In a bewildered manner he explains to the judges why he has brought his wife to court. "I don't understand what happened to us. We are married thirty-five years, and we never had trouble or complaints. I always gave her money for the table, and I paid for the gas and electricity. We had two nice children. They grew up— my daughter is a teacher in Long Island and expecting a child, my son is a student in college. Everything was all right. A year or so ago my wife got a part-time job in a bakery, she should have some extra money. Fine. I never asked her what she earned. Suddenly, without any warning, she stops living with me, she walks out on me."

"When did this happen?" says the judge.

"Almost two months ago. When I got home one evening, I found the apartment empty. My wife is gone, my son is gone, half the furniture is gone."

"Did you try to get together with your wife?"

"At first I didn't even know where she was. Then I got a letter from her, some apartment building called Rochedale Village. I called her and asked her to come back home, but she wouldn't come. So I'm here today in court."

"You want to live with her again?"

"Yes. I never had trouble with her. I want to come together. I can't figure out how everything happened against me."

The spectators in court are full of sympathy for him and full of anger at his hardhearted wife when she steps forward to tell her story.

"Mrs. Lubin," the judge begins gravely, "was it nice to walk out on your husband so suddenly? Whatever you may have against him, shouldn't you have talked it over with him first?"

"Talked it over!" she says. "What have I done for years except talk it over? Ten years already I've been wanting to move out of that apartment. The building is awful, the neighborhood has run down badly, in our block we're practically the only white people. Always my husband said we didn't have enough money to move. We had plenty money to move, but he was the only one working, so I gave in. Two years ago, when my son started college, I went out and got a job. And again I mentioned to my husband that I wanted to move. He said the place we were in was a bargain, where else could we find such a cheap rent? I said it was old and falling apart, we were entitled to a modern apartment. He said this *was* a modern apartment, because didn't it have gas and electricity? I told him I would die if I stayed there any longer, and since the money was no problem anymore I would now start looking for a new place. That was when he stopped listening to me."

"What do you mean he stopped listening to you?"

"I mean what I say. He shut up his ears, he made up his mind he wouldn't listen. I went around to look at apartments after work. I came home and told him what I saw. He didn't answer, it was like talking to the wall.

Finally I found a co-op in a nice section, a placed called Rochedale Village, that was just right for us. I told him what the price was and asked him to pay it in. He didn't answer. I have my own savings, so I paid in the price myself. I told him when I did it, I never hid anything from him. No answer. I told him on what date we had to move. I talked and talked—my son talked and talked. He never answered. When I received mail from Rochedale Village, I left it on the table, it was there for him to look at. I told him when I hired the moving company. During Passover, when I was not working, I asked him to come with me to look for new furniture. Positively no answer."

"But when the day for moving came around, he surely had something to say then?"

"You think so? That morning, when he was leaving for work, I told him we wouldn't be there when he got back. He shut the door—it was like I hadn't said a word. So my son and I moved out to the new place. A few days later he called up and said, 'Where are you?' I said, 'You know where we are, and there's a bed here waiting for you.' He hung up the phone, and the next thing I received a letter to appear in court."

The judges turn back to Mr. Lubin. "Your wife claims she told you all about the new apartment for months ahead of time. Is that true?"

"She is gone, and I want her back," Mr. Lubin says.

"Yes, but is it true that she told you all about—"

"Why did she leave? Why won't she come back? I don't understand what happened."

The judge's question seems to have brought on another one of Mr. Lubin's attacks of deafness. So they turn away from him and make their decision. They recognize that Mrs. Lubin's tactics weren't precisely kosher and that an ordinary court of law would probably tell her to move back with her husband or give up expecting any support from him. But they know that you can't budge a mountain with conventional methods. They order Mr. Lubin to move into the co-op with his wife and son and to continue paying his share of the expenses.

They announce this decision in a very loud voice. If Mr. Lubin hears it, he gives no sign. But a few days later Mrs. Lubin calls up Mrs. Richman and reports that her husband is living with her again.

Stinginess seems to be a much less common phenomenon among wives. They are given instead to a different though equally virulent disease—suspicion. It doesn't matter how long they have lived with their husbands or how faithfully their husbands have supported them; as soon as money is involved, they are ready to believe the worst. After years of happy marriage Mr. Lishner wants to put his and his wife's savings in a joint account, with both of them having the right of withdrawal. Mrs. Lishner objects strenuously. "His signature on my checks," she says, "somehow doesn't smell nice." Another wife insists that her husband has $40,000 that he hasn't told her about. When the judge asks her what proof she has of this, she answers, "How do I know that today is Wednesday or that red is red? I just know. I know what people are like." And another wife brings her husband to court because he danced with a woman at a party, "and this woman has greater assets than mine!"

This lady can't be totally blamed for her suspicions.

In this world of constant financial insecurity men do marry women who have more money than they have, in the hope of freeing themselves from anxiety. Here is a man's description of how he got together with his second wife: "I moved into one of the small hotels in Coney Island, and she got into a conversation with me. After a while she proposed marriage to me. I told her that I was unable to get married because of financial circumstances, and she told me she would take care of me and that she was not a poor girl. I reconsidered and thought it would be a good idea to get married."

Such marriages often end up in the court. The "rich" wife knows what her husband's motives were. She feels that she has conferred a supreme favor on him, and she seldom hesitates to tell him so. "I paid for everything," says one such wife to the judges. "I gave his children the nicest presents from my money. I took him to Florida, and I have all the receipts to prove how much it cost me. I supported him from the first day we were married. He had better treatment than the President." In return for the "treatment" what this particular wife wants is total subservience.

Sometimes it is hard to decide which party to feel sorry for. Consider the classic case of Hyman Zuckerman. He was a widower in his fifties, and he wanted to make his last years comfortable. He met a rich woman who told him frankly about her bank accounts, her bonds, her houses, and suggested that he would never have to work again if he married her. Zuckerman jumped at the chance, but the lady turned out to be quite different than he had expected. She was tightfisted, possessive, and tyrannical. She made him go back to work, she kept hold of all the money and doled it out to him in driblets, she nagged him and yelled at him, she was insanely jealous of him and wouldn't let him go anywhere by himself. Finally he couldn't stand it and walked out on her. She hauled him before the court, demanding that he either live with her or pay her alimony. He couldn't afford alimony, so he went back to live with her.

After a year or so, it all got too much for him again. He left her, she hauled him before the court, the case repeated itself. "We are not compatible," he said to the judges. "I want a divorce." But again the judges could do nothing; he was her legal spouse and legally bound to live with her or pay alimony. He went back to her, then he ran away again, then he came to the court again, then he went back to her. This continues off and on for sixteen years. He is a familiar figure in the court; the judges come to know his hard-luck story by heart.

At last he wears her down. Even her stubbornness and cruelty have their limits, and she gives him the divorce. When he gets the final papers, he celebrates, and a few days later he hears that his ex-wife has just died. She has no family, and he would have been the heir to her whole estate—except that he isn't her husband anymore.

Next to money the chief cause of marital troubles in this community is interfering relations. The records of the court are full of in-laws whose penchant for butting in is the reason, or the excuse, for a failing marriage.

Mr. Auerbach tells this story to the judges: "My brother-in-law has come to live with us, and he and my wife play cards every night in my house. When I say every night, I mean seven nights a week. I don't play cards. Once I said to my brother-in-law, 'How about giving me a night or two to be with my wife and take her some place.' With that he said, 'I will take it up with my sister.' This hurt me terribly."

The judges decide that Auerbach's brother-in-law has two weeks to find an apartment of his own, but Mrs. Auerbach refuses to accept this decision. "I will not give up my brother for this man," she cries. "My brother and I were together in the concentration camp. If Hitler could not separate us, Auerbach never will!"

And there is really nothing the judges can do. Auerbach leaves the court moaning, "If it wasn't enough I had a wife to cope with, God sent me a brother-in-law too!"

Mr. and Mrs. Bronston are in their thirties, have been married for seven years, and have no children. Mr. Bronston has come to court to complain about his wife's friendship with an elderly lady, Mrs. Nangler, who lives in the neighborhood.

"This woman is always around," he says. "She interferes in our lives. My wife is only happy when this woman is there. My wife never remembers my birthday, but she sends gifts to Mrs. Nangler and her family. She won't get up in the morning to prepare anything, she never cleans the apartment, she is always at this woman's house. I tell you, gentlemen, I have a wife in name only."

Bronston sounds a bit crotchety, and the spectators are inclined to dismiss his complaint as a gross exaggeration. Then Mrs. Bronston appears; she is a pretty girl who looks much younger than her years.

"Now tell us, Mrs. Bronston," says the judge, "what is this story of Mrs. Nangler?"

"It is no story," Mrs. Bronston says. "Mrs. Nangler knows me since I was a child. When my mother passed away, I lived with Mrs. Nangler until I got married. He claims that I am always in her house, but this is not true. A friend likes to visit her friend's house, and that is why I go there."

"Suppose that, in order to keep your happy union together, it would be necessary for you to devote a little more time to him instead of Mrs. Nangler—"

"This would *not* be necessary," she says in a very reasonable tone of voice. "When one marries, does one have to give up one's friends?"

"But if you are devoting more attention to her than to your husband—"

"I am not."

"But he *thinks* you are. So if that is the chief cause of his complaint against you, why isn't it important for you to see less of Mrs. Nangler?"

"I don't see it that way," she says, her voice growing a bit more agitated. "In my opinion—"

Suddenly there is an interruption. A wizened but energetic old lady stands up from among the spectators and screams out at the judges, "I am his mother! I am here to express my thoughts! I just got over a heart attack, but I had to come here for my son! She is up at Mrs. Nangler's constantly—"

The judges, with Bronston's embarrassed help, persuade the elder Mrs. Bronston to sit down again and let the hearing take its course. Then the rabbi turns back to Bronston's wife.

"Your first obligation is to your husband as against the whole world. If someone is standing between you and your husband, if your unwillingness to give up Mrs. Nangler is the cause of a breakup in your marriage, wouldn't you be willing to give her up?"

Her agitation grows. "I left him once in the first year of our marriage! He chased me from the house! He threw my bag down into the street!"

Bronston speaks up. "I did it because there were bedbugs and she had nothing in the house. She was neglecting everything—"

"All right," says the judge, "we can always find fault, but we can also find a way to make a home a home instead of a battle. Mrs. Bronston, I'm sure this woman doesn't want you two to be unhappy. Don't you think she would tell you to go to your home and make your husband happy?"

"He hasn't told you," Mrs. Bronston says, "that when I misplaced my keys a couple of week ago I couldn't get into the house, and the special policeman wouldn't recognize me because he didn't have my name listed—"

"Mrs. Bronston, are you or aren't you willing to give up Mrs. Nangler?"

Mrs. Bronston is in tears.

"No! I wouldn't give her up. I wouldn't give up a mother."

What more can the judges do? They recommend marriage counseling.

Sometimes a mother-in-law doesn't even have to be alive to go on interfering.

Another leading cause of marital disputes in this court is jealousy. Infidelity—the act, at least, not necessarily the thought—is rare in this community. As one falsely suspected husband put it, "With my troubles, my bank account, and my weak health—so that's all I need, to run around with other women!"

The rarity of the act, because of its inconvenience and its prohibitive expense, makes the frequency of the accusation all the more striking. The records of the court abound with jealous husbands and wives who clearly don't have a leg to stand on, yet no amount of logic or common sense seems able to dispel their delusion. As an example of how tenacious this delusion can be against all the evidence, here is a bit of dialogue from a case:

| | |
|---|---|
| JUDGE: | Do you and your husband work in the same place? |
| MRS. GOLUB: | Yes, as dressmakers. |
| JUDGE: | You see each other at work and go home together? |
| MRS. GOLUB: | Yes. |
| JUDGE: | Does he have dinner with you? |
| MRS. GOLUB: | Yes. |
| JUDGE: | Does he take you out to the movies? |
| MRS. GOLUB: | Yes. |
| JUDGE: | Does he ever go out at night by himself? |
| MRS. GOLUB: | No. |

JUDGE: Then when does he have time to do all this that you accuse him of doing?

MRS. GOLUB: So what? He has three illegitimate children from a gentile! I know this for a fact!

Mrs. Davidoff describes her husband's jealous behavior: "This year I got a bite from a mouse. It came into my bed. I had to go to the doctor. My husband told me I wasn't going to a doctor, I was having an affair with the Chinaman next door."

The judges arrive at the perfect solution. Mrs. Davidoff is to take her husband to the doctor's office first thing next morning; they are to question the doctor's nurse and examine his appointment book and thus establish once and for all that Mrs. Davidoff really did visit him on the day in question.

The next afternoon Ruth Richman calls Mrs. Davidoff and asks her how the judges' suggestion worked. Does her husband still believe she is having an affair with the Chinese man next door?

"Not anymore," says Mrs. Davidoff. "Now he tells me I'm having an affair with the doctor."

Mr. Hertz is Jewish, and his wife, Catholic. She doesn't practice her religion, and though she has never converted to Judaism, she has celebrated all the holidays with her husband throughout the twenty-three years of their marriage. They have had no children, but they have been happy together.

Suddenly Mrs. Hertz gets the idea that her husband is having an affair with a girl who works in his real estate office. The girl, Bliss Kupfermann, is also a Catholic married to a Jew. Mr. Hertz denies that he is having an affair. He sees his whole marriage being destroyed by his wife's obsession. Finally, when she threatens to commit suicide, he insists that she come with him to the Jewish court.

He begins his testimony with great emotion: "I swear to God, and I swear to you gentlemen, that I have been faithful to her at all times! I love her. Our marriage has been so happy. I can't believe this nightmare that has happened to me."

"Do you know a Bliss?" the judge asks.

"She is a young lady I hired for my real estate business. She left about six or eight weeks ago. Because of this situation I had to let her go."

"Have you seen her since she left your employ?"

"Positively not."

Mrs. Hertz burst in, "Whatever he swears, I know the truth. For months he threw everything at me to keep me busy. I knew her husband was flying somewhere on a trip, and the rush was to keep me occupied."

"But how can you know this, Mrs. Hertz?"

"Suspicious things were happening. The week before Christmas my bell was out of order and I think he had something to do with it. He has coded messages. I feel he's afraid of getting old. In his real estate business he rents apartments to youngsters—two or three girls at a time. He feels I'm a drag on him." She shakes her head, and her voice takes on a puzzled quality. "Maybe it's my imagination . . ." Then her voice gets firm again. "I still think Bliss is working for him. My telephone bills have been exorbitant, and most of the calls are to New Jersey, and she lives in New Jersey."

"Mr. Hertz," says the judge, "have you made calls to New Jersey?"

"Her sister and brother-in-law live in Union City," Hertz says. "Since this situation began, she calls them up every day."

"I have all kinds of other evidence," says Mrs. Hertz. "I keep a file. I call it my nonsense file—excuse me, that's what my husband calls it. And every time I would come to the office I would see what goes on. It would be Blissy this and Blissy that."

Wearily Hertz puts in, "I tried to explain to my wife that I didn't mean anything. Everyone in the office speaks that way. This girl was a terrific saleslady, and everything she sold I would get an over-ride on. Since she left we've had a man, but he can't take her place. But this doesn't mean we had an affair."

The rabbi-judge turns to Mrs. Hertz. "I think you're making something out of nothing. It seems to me that your husband is a fine man. Obviously he adores you."

The puzzled look is on Mrs. Hertz's face again. "He's a fabulous salesman. I think I am green-eyed with jealousy . . ." But then the look goes away, and she has pulled a piece of paper out of her pocketbook. "Look at this! Look at this paper please! I found this in his coat pocket only this morning. What can it be except a communication from Bliss, in code?"

The judges look at the paper. It is the letter that Ruth Richman sent to Mr. Hertz giving him instructions on how to get downtown to the Educational Alliance.

"Mrs. Hertz," says the rabbi-judge, "believe me when I tell you there is no hidden meaning in this piece of paper. It was sent to your husband from our office. There is nothing in it to fear."

"If there is nothing in it . . ." Mrs. Hertz begins. She breaks off, shaking her head slowly.

"To ease your mind," says the rabbi, "maybe you should go to a doctor. Mrs. Richman can give you the name of a good one."

"Yes, that's what I should do," Mrs. Hertz says slowly and thoughtfully. "It's me. I know it's me. What I need is a doctor."

The rabbi's suggestion is put in the form of an official decision. Then Mr. Hertz awkwardly takes his wife's arm and helps her out of the courtroom.

The records tell us no more about this case, except for one brief preliminary report from the psychiatrist to Ruth Richman. He writes that he has seen Mrs. Hertz for the first time and that she seems cooperative and plans to come again. In this first visit she mentioned that she often picks up the phone and hears words that she thinks her husband is saying to Bliss. The words she hears most often are "baby" and "flowers."

Occasionally, of course, the jealous spouse isn't being paranoid at all.

Mr. Dreyfuss, married for thirty-three years and the father of four children, suddenly becomes a playboy. He buys the latest fashions in elegant men's clothes, he comes home at four in the morning, he dyes his hair, he spends $1000 at Arthur Murray's for dance lessons. Naturally his wife suspects him of having an affair with another woman. When she accuses him of this, he doesn't deny it but tells her it would do her good to get herself a man. One night, instead of going with her to her cousin's wedding, he goes off to a B'nai B'rith dinner-dance. He claims he has to see his lawyer, who will be there. Mrs. Dreyfuss follows him to the dinnerdance. At the door she is told that Mr. and Mrs. Dreyfuss have already arrived.

"I went inside," Mrs. Dreyfuss says, "and a woman sat there with him. I tapped the woman on the shoulder and asked her if she was Mrs. Dreyfuss and she said she was. He dropped the spoon from his mouth. She got up and told me not to make a scandal, she said that he had told her his wife was sick and couldn't have any sex. The next day I ordered him out of the apartment. He says he can't afford two places, so I should let him sleep on a bed in the living room. He says that I have no right to be upset, because he is in love with this woman and I am too old for him anyway."

Dreyfuss now testifies in his defense. He is wearing one of those elegant suits his wife mentioned, and has a flower in his buttonhole. He hardly seems crushed under the consciousness of his sin.

"Have you any explanation for that B'nai B'rith dinner, Mr. Dreyfuss?" asks the judge. "Can you tell us why you were there with another woman?"

"It's simple," Dreyfuss answers. "A friend of mine asked me if I wanted to take my wife to the affair. I said I would much rather take my girlfriend. So I went there with this lady, and she paid for her own ticket. My wife tried to spy on me. A friend of mine who is a lawyer told me I wasn't committing a crime. Her spying was the crime."

"I understand you want to go on living in the apartment with your wife while you're seeing this other woman!"

"Well, naturally. It's my apartment. I'm paying the rent. Why shouldn't I come and go as I please? If I want to go dancing, I can go dancing."

"Is it true she asked this other woman if she was Mrs. Dreyfuss and this woman said that she was?"

"I didn't hear this," says Dreyfuss.

"Did you ever introduce her as your wife?"

"Not exactly."

"How many times do you take her out?"

"Two or three times a week we go to a dance."

"And you have never introduced her as Mrs. Dreyfuss?"

"It's hard to remember some things."

"I don't understand," puts in another judge, "how you wish to go on living at home under the present circumstances?"

"Why not? Is there something for me to be ashamed of? I'm a human being. I have to go out and have a little fun."

The judges order Mr. Dreyfuss to move out of the apartment at once and to keep on paying his wife her regular weekly allowance. He is amazed and rather hurt. He just can't understand how they can take such an unreasonable attitude.

Mr. Dreyfuss's complacent view of his own infidelity does not seem to be typical of this community. Illicit sexual relations before or after marriage are generally frowned upon. The Dreyfusses of this community may enjoy their peccadilloes thoroughly today, but they are likely to pay for them with strong feelings of guilt tomorrow.

Norman Feldspan, a husband and father in his fifties, a respected and well-to-do member of the community, comes to court with charges against Mrs. Nellie Brasch.

"This lady is persecuting me," Feldspan says, "and I want you to make her stop."

"Tell us about it, please."

"Twenty-one years ago I was chairman of the board of the Rabbi Solomon Panitz Yeshiva in Brooklyn. This woman's child was enrolled there. She approached me under the pretext of having me help her get her husband to this country from South America. Actually she was pursuing me."

"So what came of that?"

"Actually I started going out with her. In fact, I spent the night with her once or twice. I didn't really want to do this, but I was very naïve."

"You were a married man at that time?"

"Actually I was."

"So why didn't you stay home and keep away from her?"

"She threatened to commit suicide, and she beat me. What could I do? For three weeks I broke off with her and she threatened to kill me."

"Is this relationship still going on?"

"Not for a long time. My wife had a nervous breakdown over this situation, so after that it stopped."

There is a touch of impatience in the judge's voice. "You had an affair and it stopped. So what do you want from us?"

"I want you to tell this woman, Mrs. Nellie Brasch, to stop tormenting me. My home life is broken up because of her. She said she would kill me if she saw me with someone else. She told me to divorce my wife. I was chairman of the board of the Rabbi Solomon Panitz Yeshiva, and when they found out about this, they fired me."

"All right, but all that happened years ago. What is Mrs. Brasch doing to you *now*?"

"I asked my son to come here with me today. He told me he didn't want to look at her, and my wife told me to go back to Nellie because I lived with her for five years."

"Mr. Feldspan, why don't you tell us what your *charges* are?"

But somehow, though Feldspan goes on talking, he never seems to come out with any specific charges. So the judges turn to Mrs. Brasch.

"It is just the opposite from what he tells you," she says.

"He hasn't told us anything," a judge mutters.

"I am the one who should have brought him here," she goes on. "What he says about us years ago is true. But it's finished a long time. I live ten blocks away, and I run into him every few months, but all of a sudden, a little while ago, he starts bothering me. He calls me at all hours and tells me to leave him alone. He is supposedly a Sabbath observer, and he calls on Saturday."

"Does his wife know about this?" the rabbi asks.

"I wrote her a letter. I explained I don't bother him. I wish he would leave me alone."

"Is it possible for you to change your residence or get an unlisted number?"

"I tried to call my children, and the telephone wouldn't work. The telephone company told me that

my phone number was transferred to Mr. Feldspan—
he called them up and said he was my husband and
gave them the orders. The telephone company asked if
I wanted to bring charges. It was Yom Kippur, so I
didn't."

"What else does he do?" asks one of the judges.

"He says he is torturing me so that I will throw
myself in the East River."

Feldspan breaks in, "I say this to her so that *she*
will stop torturing *me*! I cannot sleep because of her.
I am unable to work because she will not let me
alone."

"Mr. Feldspan," says the judge, "if this woman
doesn't want any communication with you, you have
to stay away from her. Isn't that right?"

"You've got it twisted around," Feldspan says. "I
do stay away from her. For the last thirteen years I
stayed away. Now *she* won't stay away."

"What is he talking about?" Mrs. Brasch cries. "I
never want to look at him again—that's all I ask out
of life!"

"Mr. Feldspan," says the rabbi, trying to keep any
trace of exasperation out of his voice, "you are a
man of fifty-five, and at that age in life a man has
certain difficulties. My advice to you is that you get
her out of your mind. Go to the Educational Alliance
in your spare time. And have you ever been to a
psychiatrist?"

"I went once to Bellevue. They gave me pills. My
son who is a lawyer said I have a legal case against
her—"

"Mrs. Richman will give you the name of a good

psychiatrist," says the rabbi. "He will help you get this woman out of your mind."

"She also ruined another man," Feldspan says. "She ruins plenty of men!" He turns fiercely on Mrs. Brasch. "Stay away from me already, will you!" And he goes out, muttering to himself.

# CHAPTER

# 9

## Husbands and Wives—Three

The final significant cause of marital disputes in this community is simple incompatibility. This is an all-purpose word covering everything that doesn't fit into any of the other categories. Husbands and wives are incompatible when they discover, for any reason or no reason, that they have developed peculiar and conflicting tastes, that they don't talk the same language anymore, that the traits they used to enjoy in each other are now unbearably irritating, that they can't imagine what they ever thought they had in common.

Sometimes this incompatibility is based on clear-cut social or cultural differences that existed before the marriage took place. Many cases concern husbands who were brought up with old European attitudes toward marriage and can never quite reconcile themselves to the very different attitudes of their American wives.

Mrs. Janovic complains to the court about her husband, Anton: "He has European tactics. He says a man is complete boss, I must report every move I make. He follows me to the beauty parlor, and I have to go with him to take a haircut in the barber shop. If I went to a Hadassah meeting, he followed me, asked me questions, and I was so embarassed I stopped going. Also, if my daughter wants to choose her clothes, he insists upon coming along, he embarrasses us in front of the saleslady. And if I don't do what he wants, he fights with me and is violent to me."

Janovic rises angrily. "I am never violent to her! My wife is a liar! From listening to all her lies it's a miracle I don't hit her!"

The judge finally has to say to him, "Please, Mr. Janovic, don't talk with your fist like that." He sits down, and at the end of the testimony the rabbi gives him a little lecture: "In Europe the wife only had to have children and work. In America you live differently. You must be practical. You must live in the light of American families."

But the old-country ways are too deeply ingrained in Mr. Janovic. Like most husbands of his type he takes it as an axiom that his wife is supposed to be a cart horse. It is almost impossible to ease such a man's sense of grievance. He brings out one last denunciation before he goes stamping out of the room: "That a woman can take her husband into a court—this is the worst thing I ever heard about America!"

Sometimes the trouble arises because of differences in education or social class. Often in the course of a marital hearing, the husband or wife will say something that clearly reveals his or her sense of superiority. A young husband announces in an injured tone, "I can never forgive her for what she called me. I was brought up in a refined home. Her parents are decidedly of a much lower standard than my parents. They talk vulgarly. I never heard a vulgar word until I married." When the judge asks him, out of curiosity, what his wife *did* call him, the young man cannot bring himself to pronounce the offensive word; he writes it down on a piece of paper and shows it to the judges.

Another husband, saddled with a socially superior wife, complains to the court, "Sometimes she talks too loud and I tell her 'Shut up!' Then she gets angry and tells me that a refined person would say 'Keep quiet!' "

Even more than language, personal cleanliness becomes a source of hostility between these mismatched couples. The young man who complained about his wife's vulgarity also said, "Her parents do not keep a clean house, nor change their clothing regularly." And the wife with a similar grievance says, "*I* am clean, I have been *taught* to be clean. My husband is only clean because I keep him clean—he never learned any better."

There is reason to suppose, of course, that these cultural and social differences are the pretexts rather than the causes for discord. Presumably these husbands and wives knew about their differences when they got married. (Very seldom does a marriage flounder because one of the parties has deliberately deceived the other ahead of time—like one husband who told his wife before the wedding that he was a newspaperman and broke it to her afterward that he had a newsstand where he sold papers.) What seems to happen is that differences that hardly mattered at the beginning of the marriage gradually become important and then crucial.

This same process takes place with couples whose social and educational backgrounds are exactly the same. If there are no special reasons for them to be at odds, they will dredge up reasons from the daily routine of their lives. A husband finds it intolerable that his wife should come to bed every night with cold cream on her face, though she has been doing it regularly for twenty-five years. A wife develops an aversion to her husband's custom of drinking a bottle of beer with his meals. A husband complains about his wife's long-standing habit of putting the vegetables on a newspaper on the floor whenever she defrosts the refrigerator.

Mrs. Rivkin, in her sixties, comes to court and asks to be separated from her husband of thirty years. None of the usual items of complaint appear on her list; she doesn't accuse him of being stingy, cruel, neglectful, or unfaithful. "So what *do* you have against him?" the judge asks.

She answers, "Mr. Rivkin always has something to say about to me. If I am reading a magazine or watching the television, he talks to me. If I go to my daughter because I get disgusted in the house with him, he calls me up there to talk to me. If I don't go to her, he makes that a subject of conversation. In the middle of the night he wakes me up because he has something else to say."

"What is it exactly that you want from Mr. Rivkin?"

"If he would only keep quiet, I wouldn't want anything, but he talks and talks and I feel terrible. If he does not keep quiet, then I want a separation because it is impossible to stay with him anymore."

"What would you want from Mr. Rivkin if he gave you a separation?"

"I would not even ask for any money. I would stay at my daughter's and she would support me."

It is impossible to determine just yet if Mrs. Rivkin has a valid complaint or if she is an excessively nervous woman. So the judges call in her husband.

"Mr. Rivkin," says the judge, "let us hear your side of the story."

"My wife wants a separation," he says. "She won't get this because there is no cause for it and I don't want it. I have tried my best all the years I have been with her. I am a messenger for a bank. May I place the case right from the start and not like Goldie placed it? She starts from the middle. I met my wife thirty years ago when I was a young man thirty-two years old—"

"Excuse me," says the judge, "but is this relevant to—"

"Before we started getting serious," Mr. Rivkin goes on, "I told my wife all about me—I told her how much money I make, my whole background. Now here is the important point. She has a cousin Willy who is a house painter. He is about the same age as I am, and he paints houses. The first week we were married he came into our apartment at seven in the morning, God knows where he got a key, and he said she asked him to come and do some painting—"

"Mr. Rivkin, what has this got to do with your wife's—"

"All right, forget about Willy." Rivkin gives a wave of his hand. "I'll skip to 1955 when I asked my wife to go

away on a vacation with me. She wanted to go to
Canada because her brother lives there. So I bought
two tickets to Canada. That day there was something
wrong with the bus, for which reason it was detained
and would not be running for quite a while. So I sent
the tickets back and said that we would go to other
places. Now the point is—"

"That's interesting, Mr. Rivkin," says the judge, "but
as to your wife's—"

"Now the point is, the next thing I knew she told me
to leave the house, and I did. I was out of the house for
six weeks, during which time I dropped from one hundred forty-eight to one hundred thirty-two pounds. Everyone asked me what happened to me, I was turning
into a skeleton—"

Mrs. Rivkin throws up her hands. "You see what I'm
telling you? He talks and talks and never says a thing!"

The judges get the point. With difficulty they persuade Mr. Rivkin to be quiet. The rabbi turns to Mrs.
Rivkin sympathetically.

"Mrs. Rivkin, is this something which is new with
him, or was he always like this?"

"Always—from the first day I knew him."

"But you married him. You lived with him thirty
years. Why, all of a sudden, does his talking bother you
so much?"

"Why? Why?" Mrs. Rivkin shakes her head, but she
can't explain anymore.

"I think," says the rabbi, "that you have forgotten
what it is to be alone. It is true, I must say with due
respect, that you have a husband who is somewhat—
talkative. But therefore I would say it is the same as if
he had a broken back. Would you leave him for that?

126

No, surely not. You would say that it is your duty to be with him and take care of him."

"After all," one of the other judges puts in, "you have some good days with him, don't you?"

"Yes," says Mrs. Rivkin, "but only when he is sick with a sore throat."

The judges talk it over and decide that the Rivkins should live together for a while and seek help from a clinic that specializes in geriatric cases.

"Mrs. Richman will find a place," says the rabbi, "and they will surely help you."

"I will do anything he should keep quiet," says Mrs. Rivkin.

The Rivkins leave. From the hall Mr. Rivkin can be heard talking.

Mr. and Mrs. Ziegler are in their thirties, have been married for ten years, and have two small children. Since childhood she has had a spinal condition that sometimes makes it difficult for her to sleep at night.

She brings her husband to court because for the last six months he has become violent and abusive in his behavior toward her and the children. "If I try to help my little girl with her work for a test, he gets perturbed. He starts hitting her."

The judge turns to Ziegler. "Mr. Ziegler, do you hit your daughter?"

Ziegler avoids the judge's eyes. "At times."

"He hits her on the head," says Mrs. Ziegler. "The poor child's head is not there anymore."

The judge says, "Mr. Ziegler, do you hit her on the *head?*"

"It all depends where I land," he says.

"He will call the children and me any names," Mrs. Ziegler says. "Bastard, bitch, fucker—it is just horrible."

"Mr. Ziegler," says the judge, "is it true that you use such language to your family?"

"Only when I am angry."

"What is your problem, Mr. Ziegler? Why do you behave this way?"

"My problem?" he says. "My problem is that at three or four o'clock in the morning I get out of bed—she is in the bathroom, sleeping on the seat. I have to wake her up."

The court psychiatrist has to speak up at this. "Why do you leave your bed in the morning, Mrs. Ziegler? Is it because you want to leave your husband?"

"I don't want to leave the bed," she says. "I have a very bad spine. It is difficult for me to lie in my bed. I can sleep better when I'm sitting up."

"How often does this happen to you?" says one of the judges.

"Two, three times a week."

"Why don't you sleep in the kitchen rather than in the bathroom?"

"Sometimes I do. But the kitchen is cold at night."

"Couldn't you raise your pillows and sleep in the bed sitting up?"

"I have done that. That is what I used to do all the time. But for six months, whenever I raise the pillows, he drags me down again. He says nobody sleeps like that, and he drags me down."

"Why do you drag her down, Mr. Ziegler? You know about your wife's physical condition, don't you?"

"I don't speak to doctors. I don't bother with them."

"Even so, you believe her, don't you, when she says it is hard for her to sleep lying down straight?"

"Yes, I believe her. But I can't get used to it. My mind can't get adjusted to this."

"You knew about this condition when you married her?"

"Yes, I knew."

"For ten years you lived with it. So why, in the last six months, does your mind have trouble adjusting?"

Ziegler just stares at the judge glumly. He can't say a word.

"Mr. Ziegler, you must put an end to this violent behavior," says the rabbi. "It is not you alone that is involved. Our hearts all cry out for your sick wife and your children. They are innocent."

In a low voice Ziegler says, "I don't want to hurt them."

The very opposite also occurs. People not only develop sudden unaccountable aversions to their mate's familiar habits, they also develop new habits, tastes, eccentricities that they never had before and destroy their marriages as a consequence.

Mrs. Lipman complains about her husband: "For twelve years we have lived together. He is a good man, he makes a good living, he treats me well. There is nothing to say against him. Two years ago he starts with the canaries."

"Starts *what* with canaries?" asks a judge.

"He has about forty canaries. He makes us crazy in the house with the noise of these birds. The children have to feed them and clean the cage."

The judges ask Mr. Lipman to explain. He makes an earnest effort. "I only took in a couple at the beginning," he says. "I kept them in my room. But they started to have birds, and there was nobody but me to look after them. I feel at home with them, with my singing birds. They give me pleasure when everyone is against me."

"But who is against you, Mr. Lipman? Your wife and your children love you. It is only the birds they are against."

"Yes. Yes, I know this. But in the old country, when I was a child, there were birds. I always had a fondness for them."

"Your wife says she will leave the house unless you get rid of these birds. Surely you don't prefer them to your wife."

"No, naturally I don't. If it's between the birds and her—all right, I will throw out the cages tomorrow. Why not?"

Mr. Lipman is silent, his shoulders hunched up, his face very white.

Mr. Denker, a real estate salesman, is forty-eight years old, his wife is forty-five, and they have two teenage children. They have been happily married for eighteen years. He takes good care of his family. He is good-tempered and affectionate, and everybody likes him. Mrs. Denker has come to court with her first serious complaint against him.

"A year ago he started this habit," she says. "He collects papers."

"What kind of papers?"

"Any kind. From the street, from garbage cans, from

everywhere. He brings home papers, torn books, wrappings from packages. He stores his papers in every room. We haven't got such a big apartment—nobody can come inside. He keeps promising to clean out his papers, but he has never done it. And if I try to touch this trash myself, he gets mad at me and accuses me of throwing out important things."

"What do you want, Mrs. Denker? Do you want a separation from him?"

"A separation—God forbid! I only want him to be a *mensch.* We just had a painting, and he promised to clean up some of his junk. He has papers from the year one. I want him to keep his promise."

"We believe you're telling the truth, Mrs. Denker," says the judge, "but don't you think—without meaning to—you might be exaggerating a little too? Many people have hobbies and enjoy collecting things. And if a wife didn't happen to be sympathetic to her husband's hobby, she might inadvertently make a bigger issue out of it than it really should be."

"That's what I expected," Mrs. Denker says. "I told myself, 'When I tell this story, nobody will believe it.' So I had my son who is sixteen take some pictures with his camera—he's a good photographer, and he took pictures of the living room in our apartment. Look at these pictures, please, and tell me who's making an issue."

She shows the judges the photographs. After a few minutes to examine them, the judges call up Mr. Denker. He is neatly dressed, personable, quiet in his manner.

"You heard what your wife said," says the judge. "What is your answer to her charges?"

"My wife is a lovely woman, but she exaggerates things. As you told her yourself, women sometimes don't like a man's hobby."

"Were these pictures taken in your home?"

Denker looks at the pictures. "Yes, the pictures are authentic. But I know a little bit about photography, and I can tell you these are enlarged and therefore distorted."

"Even if the reality is only half what we see here . . ." begins the judge, but he can't bring himself to finish.

"Honestly, Mr. Denker," says the rabbi-judge, "if someone wanted to sit down in your home, where could they sit with all that stuff around?"

"You're making a mountain out of a molehill," Denker says. "When I get these papers sorted out and filed away—"

"Why do you do this?" a judge interrupts. "What got you started anyway?"

"I got started, that's all. One day I saw some papers, and I said, 'This is very interesting, it's a pity to throw this away.' So I got started. What's so terrible about it? I know I have my faults. Nobody is perfect. But people do a lot worse things than collect interesting papers."

"This is a very aggravating problem," says a judge. "You don't live in a home. You live in a junkyard."

"We know you're a sincere man and a good husband," says the rabbi. "People have a right to their hobbies. But people must also think of others."

The judges confer, and then the rabbi says, "It is our decision that you should get rid of the papers. If you don't do this within a week, Mrs. Denker has the right to separate from you, and you will have to pay for the support of her and the children."

"This is a terrible decision," says Denker. "I love my wife and my children. I can't live apart from them."

"Then throw away the papers."

"I have spent over a year collecting those papers. If I throw them away, what have I got?

The judges are unmoved. They call for the next case.

The following morning Denker calls up Mrs. Richman at her office. He wants to know if the decision can be set aside, if he can make an appeal, if he can have another hearing. "Is this supposed to be Jewish conciliation?" he asks. "My wife gives up nothing, I give up everything!"

"All you give up are the papers," says Mrs. Richman.

There is no answer at the other end of the phone. A moment later Mrs. Richman can hear him hanging up.

The cases just described illustrate a phenomenon that is so frightening as to be almost unbearable. It can happen that one or the other partner in a marriage (or sometimes each at the same time) will suddenly begin to feel that he is entirely alone. As if by magic, the person he married has been whisked off the face of the earth, and he finds himself trapped in a sealed room with a total stranger.

This effect of total alienation from each other is expressed over and over again in certain telltale phrases that married couples use in court. A wife says, "We are living at the present time under the same roof, but not together in the same world." A husband says, "When I don't talk to her, she asks me what I am hiding. When

I do talk to her, she says she can't understand what I say." A wife says, "He takes me out, he talks to me, but he does not *see* me. I am not there. I am his fifth wheel, not his wife." And a husband says, "I am a boarder in the house!" To which his wife replies, "You make yourself a boarder."

All these remarks are just so many cries for help against the terrible negation, the plague of emptiness, that devastates so many marriages that are brought to the court. This negation cannot be explained entirely in rational terms. We seldom get the feeling that it has been created deliberately or willfully. The "total stranger" seems to be even more of a victim than his unfortunate partner whose world he can no longer share. His incomprehensible metamorphosis is the symptom of some dreadful virus—of loneliness, of estrangement—that comes out of nowhere to strike men down. At the heart of every troubled marriage—and the court's experience surely bears this out—there is a mystery.

It is characteristic of the court to recognize this mystery, to feel the proper awe in its presence, but at the same time to have hopes of solving it. Underneath all their pious exhortations and complacent lectures, the judges hold definite views, rooted in Jewish tradition, of what a happy marriage is and how it might be achieved.

The marriage will be successful if the man is tough-minded, strong, and self-reliant. He must not let himself be dominated. He must be the breadwinner for the family, distributing his earnings generously and fairly but firmly, according to his own judgment. He must be the king in the house. The woman must be warm, patient, and wise. She is permitted to get her way, but she must not *seem* to be getting her way. She must remember the old Jewish proverb that some of the judges are fond of quoting: "A smart wife says, 'If you want to be the head, I will be the neck.'" In return for her tact and self-effacement, she must receive consideration, honor, and even a kind of worship. She must be the queen in the house.

Women's Lib would probably not approve, but the men and women who appear before this court do not seriously question these basic assumptions. Besides, in the characteristic fashion of Jewish assumptions, there is a loophole. Having laid down these exalted principles to guide the relations between the sexes, the judges never hesitate, in any specific case, to push the virtues of compromise.

"I give her honor and respect," says an indignant husband, "and what does she give me? Every night boiled beef!"

"Don't you like boiled beef?" asks the judge.

"Certainly I like it. But every night?"

"Marriage is a give-and-take proposition," says the judge. "If you like boiled beef, you can live with it."

The king and queen, in short, should know their royal prerogatives, but they shouldn't look too closely at how those prerogatives are being maintained. The price of liberty is eternal vigilance, but if liberty was what you wanted, why did you get married?

# CHAPTER

# 10

# *Parents*

In dealing with the relations between parents and children, the court's attitude is clear-cut: A parent's love for a child is not only sacred but imperishable. This love exists independently of the child's intrinsic worth, moral or otherwise; the parent must forgive the child even when God can't. In marital disputes where children are involved, this belief motivates many of the judges' decisions. It has been noted that the judges rarely recommend divorce to an unhappy couple; if the couple has children, this recommendation is even rarer. As a judge put it once to such a couple, "Here are two children who need the love of a mother and father. These two children must be protected. This is the duty of every mother and father in any race or religion. I am interested *only* in these children."

On another occasion, when a dispute between a mother and her son ended happily, a judge cried out almost in ecstasy, "A mother and son should embrace! I am glad you two have done so. There is nothing like a mother's embrace and a kiss from a son. If a mother and son embrace, everything will be all right!"

We may smile at the naïveté. How, in the second half of the twentieth century, can anyone have such unqualified faith that the bond between parent and child is a blessing? We have all read *King Lear,* not to mention *Portnoy's Complaint.* Nevertheless, the records of the court contain any number of indications that the judge may have a point—at least sometimes.

Six children, ranging in age from twelve to twenty-three, all live together in the same house with their parents. The atmosphere, as the testimony reveals, is horrifying. There are constant insults, bullying, screaming, outbreaks of physical violence. The judges finally suggest that some of the children had better move out of the house. Instantly the whole family is shocked, and the mother, speaking for all of them, cries out, "What do you mean, my children should live among strangers? People who don't love them and care about them?"

In the heat of a violent dispute with his older daughter, a father mentions that his youngest daughter was once sent to reform school. The older daughter turns on him furiously, "This is something to be kept to ourselves! This is not something for the whole world to know! I thought you had some family feeling!" Her astonishment seems odd, considering that she has just been accusing her father of the most outrageous acts against his family, but he accepts her rebuke without a word and hangs his head in shame.

A wife asks the court for a separation on the grounds that her husband has a violent temper and frequently beats their twelve-year-old son. The boy himself is called in; he confirms his mother's charges and gives horrendous details of the beatings. The judges ask him if he would like to see his parents separated, and the boy answers vehemently. "No, no! I want him to stop hitting me, but I don't want him to leave! He's my father!"

"But you have such a bad relationship," says the judge.

"That isn't true," says the boy. "Except that he beats me, we have a very good relationship."

There does seem to be *something* about the parent-child bond that transcends the simple, often brutal facts. Whatever it is, the judges believe in it. In case after case they implement this belief in many different ways.

Mrs. Brimberg, who is Mr. Brimberg's second wife, feels that his grown children by his first marriage treat her with contempt. Her husband insists on having them over to the house every Sunday, at which time they insult her or ignore her or look down their noses at her. She wants the court to order her husband not to make her entertain his children in his house anymore.

The judges hardly even consider Mrs. Brimberg's charges against her stepchildren. They content themselves with advising Mr. Brimberg to tell his children that his wife must be respected. They devote most of their decision to what they clearly consider to be the important point: under no circumstances are Mr. Brimberg's children to be kept out of his house. Regardless of how they act toward her, the stepmother must invite them and entertain them. To get between a father and his children is a greater sin, in the eyes of the judges, than to get between a man and his wife.

One of Mrs. Isaac's complaints against her husband is that he never eats with the children. In his defense Mr. Isaacs says, "It is bad for my digestion. There is such a tumult at the table. As long as there is no tumult, I would do it."

"Is it not a happy tumult?" asks the judge, and Mr. Isaacs is ordered to eat with the children.

This feeling that the bond between parent and child is sacred extends to grandparents too.

Mr. and Mrs. Osterman, in their sixties, had a daughter, Lenore, who was married for five years to Roger Levine. Several years ago Lenore died, and Levine remarried. He moved to a suburb of Newark, New Jersey, set up practice as a dentist, and, of course, brought his two small sons by his first marriage to live with him. His new wife had also been married before; her husband had died, leaving her with three children.

Now the Ostermans have brought their former son-in-law to the court, charging that he won't let them come to visit their grandchildren. Listening to their side of the story, we can't help feeling that Levine and his second wife are monsters.

"We went out about two weeks ago to see the children in New Jersey," says Osterman. "We had received instructions not to come, but my wife wanted to see our daughter's children, so we came anyway. We saw the littlest one, the three-year-old boy, Ronnie, playing in the yard. My wife kissed him. He told us that the older brother, his brother Danny, was in school. Since we couldn't come in to the house, we went to the school and watched to see Danny come out. But we missed him, we heard that he went home already. So we went to the house again, and she was waiting for us, Mrs. Levine, and she said to us, 'You will not see him!' When we got a glimpse of the boy, he turned his head away and ran away because he did not want to see us. I don't know the reason why they won't let us see the boy."

"I was told not to come," says Mrs. Osterman, on the verge of tears, "because I am not the grandmother. My son-in-law has parents, and his wife has parents, and those are the real grandparents, they told me. Danny used to love me, I used to call him, but then they got an unlisted phone."

"You objected to your son-in-law marrying again?" asks the judge.

"No, I was not against him marrying again. He has been a good father to my grandchildren, and I knew it would be good they should also have a mother. But why have they withdrawn the children from me?"

The judges, rather shocked, ask the Levines why they are doing this to the children's grandparents.

"It is a very difficult situation," Levine begins. His manner is neither arrogant nor cold-blooded. It is obvious that he feels all this deeply. "I feel that they may harm the children mentally if they see them. Every time she sees them she says, 'Regards from your mother. She is alive, and she sent me here.' Danny is a smart, intelligent boy, and when she says this he gets mixed up.

"Also there are not only *two* children involved. There are five children. My wife also had children from her past husband, and they are considered part of the family. The last time Mrs. Osterman saw them, a year ago, she insulted my wife's children. She brought Danny a radio, and pointing to my wife's three children she said, 'Do not let them use it.'"

Mrs. Levine speaks up for the first time. She is a small, delicate-looking woman. "I told Danny's teacher that I am not the real mother," says Mrs. Levine, "but this he doesn't like to hear me say. His teacher read me a composition he wrote entitled 'If I Had One Million Dollars.' 'If I had a million dollars,' he wrote, 'I would give four hundred dollars to the Boy Scouts, one hundred dollars to the temple, and the rest to my mother.' I think I am doing a good job raising the children. My neighbors tell me I am doing a good job."

"Mr. and Mrs. Levine," says a judge, "What about a compromise? Do you have any objections to the children going to their grandparents' home?"

"Why would that be any better?" Levine says. "what would stop her from telling them terrible things and crying over them about the dead mother? It would be worse if my wife or I weren't there."

The case poses a difficult problem for the judges. They understand perfectly how the Levines feel; it can't be denied that the old people's behavior is impossible. Yet there is a principle at stake too. Family continuity must somehow be maintained, even at the cost of the children's temporary discomfort and the parents' wounded pride. So the judges ask the Ostermans to leave the room, and then make a concerted effort to persuade the Levines to let bygones be bygones.

The rabbi-judge begins. "You are young people and of today's world. These people are old. They are hurt by what happened to their daughter. These people have pain and react emotionally and are the next day sorry for what they say. I would suggest, because you are young and intelligent, forget any insults, overlook certain things. Be understanding, create a little love, give them some pleasure."

"They insult my three children," says Mrs. Levine.

And Levine adds, "She called and said that Danny needs dental work and that I should not do anything for the other children as they are not mine."

"We cannot endow these grandparents with enough intellect," says a judge, "to accept the other three children as much as their daughter's two. We too would like them to accept all five, but we cannot see how this is possible and how you can expect them to understand. Therefore you must have compassion, no matter how many times you are stepped on."

"In other words," Levine says, "we should overlook everything."

"When you have compassion," says the rabbi-judge "this will translate itself through you to your children. You want them to grow up compassionate people, don't you?"

"Let us say that I start now, and *they* forget and step over the line again?"

"We are not trying to overburden you," says the judge. "We just want you to give them a chance."

The Levines look anguished, but they finally give in. They agree to take the children on regular visits to their grandparents.

Now the judges call the Ostermans back in. They explain what the Levines are willing to do and deliver a tactful lecture on how to behave properly with the children. "You should always have a happy appearance, and you should not speak to them about the deceased. You can never win them with tears. Do you understand this, and will you do this?"

"Yes, we'll do it." Mr. Osterman says. "We'll always speak to them happily."

"With my own grandchildren," says Mrs. Osterman, "I can't mention the name of my beloved daughter?"

The rabbi ignores this and goes on with the lecture. "One other thing. These two are the children of your daughter, but now they are the brothers of three other children. You must remember that, and you must not say things against their brothers and sisters."

Mrs. Osterman begins to protest. "How can I make no difference? The other three are not on the same level—"

"We understand," says Mr. Osterman, firmly taking hold of his wife's arm. "Don't worry."

So the decision is made official. The old people leave, and the Levines follow. But not before Levine has given a shake of his head and said, "They will never do it. You don't know them the way I do."

Does the court assume that there are no bad parents, no people who *ought* to be separated from their children?

The court's view on this question tends to be ambivalent. It certainly encounters many parents who seem to oppress or neglect their children with no apparent awareness that they are trampling on a sacred principle. But dreadful as these parents are, the court's tendency is to assume that they are redeemable. Unless it can be proved otherwise, every human being is presumed to have the instinct of parenthood deep down inside of him somewhere.

Acting on this assumption, the judges will often spend a lot of time digging for that instinct. Mr. Rosenblum, after his wife's death, refuses to give his twenty-two-year-old daughter the money that his wife asked him to give her. He doesn't deny that the request was made by his wife on her death bed, but nothing was put down on paper, and so the law can't force him to part with a penny. "Let the girl beg for it," he says, "she still won't get it." Rosenblum seems incorrigible. But the judges probe and finally come up with the truth. His daughter is going out with a boy, and Rosenblum is frightened that she will get married and leave him alone. His love for his daughter and his fear of loneliness are the causes of his behavior. The judges explain this carefully to the girl and assure Rosenblum that she loves him and won't turn away from him even if she does get married, and he agrees to give her the money.

But even when the parent *does* turn out to be a monster, the judges will probably not recommend separation from the children. The theory is that the act of separation is an affront to nature and to God, far more monstrous in itself than any circumstances that might lead up to it and dangerously likely to infect and corrupt the people who commit it.

And it must be admitted that this theory is constantly being confirmed by cases before the court. Dr. Peter Holstein, for instance, was rejected and ignored by his father all through his childhood. "My father was a man who didn't care to listen to people or talk to people. My problem with him has always been communication. If I asked him what day it was, he would say, 'Someday I

will tell you.' Every question I ever asked him he answers, 'Go away, I have nothing to say.' Since I was
seven years old my father has had nothing to say." As
soon as he was old enough to leave home, Holstein cut
all his ties with his father, and he is just as adamant
today, twenty years later, when the old man brings him
to court to ask for a reconciliation.

The judges can make no headway with Dr. Holstein,
and finally they have to dismiss the case, but one significant fact emerges in the course of the testimony. Dr.
Holstein has a son of his own, Robbie, who is sixteen.
Robbie would like his father and grandfather to get
together. He tells the judges that he has often spoken
to his father about this. "But my father won't listen to
me. He just doesn't pay attention to what I say to him.
That's the trouble, we can't communicate."

Though the judges subscribe to the principle that
there are no "bad" parents, they recognize that many
parents do great damage to their children. The damage
occurs not because parents love their children too little
but because they love them too much. Every human
virtue carries with it its own characteristic danger. The
"everything for the children" attitude often leads to
possessiveness, to the excessive care and anxiety that
smothers its object. This feeling is at the heart of many
of the parent-child disputes that come before the court.
It is very difficult, almost impossible, to root out. This
doesn't stop the judges from trying, of course.

Saul Glazer, who is forty-four years old, is separated
from his wife and is going around with a divorcée
whom he met in the laundromat that his mother owns
and he manages. His mother has become hysterical

about this. She tells the judges triumphantly that she has tried to kill herself—"I took eighteen pills!" She also threatens to kill Saul and the divorcée, "and for myself, afterwards, I have still some pills left!"

Saul has brought her to court in the hope that the judges can talk some sense into her. "I feel that you can advise my mother that her forty-four-and-a-half-year-old son should be emancipated. Right now I live under her tutelage. This is what wrecked my marriage, and now she is wrecking me again. Of course," he adds, "I know that I am to blame too. I work in my mother's business. I eat in her home. We have been living in the same apartment house for eleven years."

The judges get nowhere with Mrs. Glazer. So they suggest to Saul that he begin his emancipation by moving to a different apartment house. This makes his mother cry out, "If I let him go, he will see that woman every day!"

"Why don't you let things take place without you?" the judge says to her. But Mrs. Glazer leaves the court muttering about pills.

Justin Eingorn works for his father, Julius, in the business of manufacturing plastic placemats. Justin has been in this business for sixteen years, and now he wants his father to make him a partner, as he promised he would do someday.

"I am a grown man, and my father can't understand that," Justin says. "I do everything in the place. I sell, I supervise the factory, I look over the accounts. I am a partner as far as work but not as far as authority."

Julius Eingorn can't bring himself to accede to his son's request. "I cannot trust him," Julius says.

"He has been with you for sixteen years," says the businessman-judge. "For a long time now you *have* trusted him."

"He is a terrible businessman," says Julius.

"If he's so terrible," says the judge, "why have you given him so much responsibility through the years?"

Julius can't answer that. He tries a different tack. "Why should he *want* to be a partner? He is drawing a big salary as it is. If I make him officially a partner, he will have to share with me the profits. His salary will stop, and he will draw less money. So doesn't this *prove* what a terrible businessman he is?"

The judges could order Julius to make his son a partner, but they realize the futility of this. Harmony between the two men is impossible while both of them are in the business together. The judges order Julius to give his son a large sum of money—a kind of separation bonus for his years of faithful service—and with this money Justin can set up a business of his own.

Marilyn Schechter, who is in her twenties, brings her mother before the court.

"Miss Schechter," says the judge, "you are single and living away from your mother?"

"Yes, I cannot get along with her."

"Where do you live?"

"I do not wish to mention it. If my mother knew the address, she would go down there and make scenes until I have to move out. She says I have no right to live away from her."

"Is this what your complaint is all about?"

"This and much more. My mother knows where I work, and she hounds me at my place of business. She has a violent temper. She throws things at me. She almost blinded me once with a belt. Every fellow I go out with is not good enough for her. She asks them their intentions immediately. At the same time she continuously calls me an old maid. She wants me to jump out the window because I am not married."

"Do you take money from your mother?"

"I am a bookkeeper. I make enough money to take care of myself and to put some aside. My mother has no understanding. I was engaged when I was nineteen, but I broke it off, and my mother screamed at me for three weeks. I cannot marry anybody I cannot get along with, but she'll never understand this."

At this point the mother—a tiny woman in her fifties who looks as if she would crumple at the first touch—begins to cry. The judges must spend a few minutes soothing away her tears before they can question her.

"Tell us, Mrs. Schechter, what is so bad about it that your daughter wants to live away from you?"

Between gulps, Mrs. Schechter answers. "My husband died eleven years ago. Marilyn was twelve. I took care of her by myself. The sacrifices I gave up for her! As time went on she got more and more apart from me. She never told me what she did. She went to school and never told me what she did there. She lied all the time."

"Children are supposed to grow apart from us as they get older," says the rabbi-judge. "Now tell us, why is it important that she live with you?"

"A year ago she went to California," says Mrs. Schechter. "I forbade her to go as the trip was too expensive and I didn't care for the girl she went with. Three weeks later she was supposed to come home, but she didn't come. A niece in New Jersey told me she was staying with her. She was there for a few months, she refused to come home. Then she moved away and nobody knew where. She wanted to be left alone."

"Yes, but what objections do you have to that? She is over twenty-one and self-supporting. She is not running around in the streets. She went to school, she learned a profession, she has tried to better herself. Why can't she live alone and come to visit you?"

Mrs. Schechter doesn't answer. She starts crying again.

"She hits me when I visit her," Marilyn says. "I almost became deaf because of her."

"How bad can she hit you?" one of the judges asks. "Look at her—she's half your size."

"When she hits me, she's not so small," Marilyn says.

Mrs. Schechter more or less stops crying again. One of the judges turns to her. "Your daughter wants to live by herself, Mrs. Schechter. Why don't you respect her wishes? And don't annoy her at her place of business— she may lose her job."

"Be nice to her," says the rabbi-judge, "and she will come to see you every week."

At this Marilyn starts crying.

"Don't cry, don't cry," says the rabbi. "The court is not ordering you to live at home. We feel you should stay where you are. Surely it isn't much to ask you should try to see her once in a while."

"She aggravates me so terribly," says Marilyn.

"Why did she use me as a sponge?" Mrs. Schechter says, her voice suddenly much louder than anybody would expect from looking at her. "Why did she let me sacrifice my life to her?"

*149*

"I did not," Marilyn says. "My opinion was never asked."

"Four years ago she broke off an engagement," says Mrs. Schechter. "Let her tell me why she never returned the ring to the boy!"

"What is this business of a ring?" says one of the judges impatiently. "It is up to her whether she returns the ring or not. We must get back to the problem at hand."

"Marilyn," says the rabbi, "why shouldn't you visit your mother this Friday? You will feel good about it if you do."

"I cannot come this Friday. I have a date."

"Next Tuesday then?"

"She doesn't treat me like a person but a dog," Marilyn says. "I'll be lucky to be alive after I visit her."

"She will treat you differently from now on. She will understand that she must give you love if she wants your love." The rabbi turns with an encouraging smile to Mrs. Schechter. "You'll promise us that, won't you, my dear lady?"

After a moment, Mrs. Schechter makes the promise. The judges are delighted. "Shake hands, kiss, be friends," they urge the mother and daughter, and soon both ladies are weeping in each other's arms. "Go home now, and live in peace," says the rabbi. Mrs. Schechter and Marilyn leave the court together.

The judges are positively beaming. They congratulate one another on their success. But a few minutes later, as they are about to start the next case, Marilyn comes running back into the room. Her eyes are red, and she gasps out, "She threatened me! She told me she would take it out on me because I don't love my mother and I bring my troubles to strangers! She gave me a hit in front of the elevator."

The judges tell Marilyn to wait a few minutes until her mother has had a chance to leave the building.

Then they set aside their disappointment and call the next case. Part of the job, they realize, is to waste as little time as possible brooding over their failures.

# CHAPTER

## 11

*Children*

Even allowing for possessiveness, jealousy, overanxiety, and a hundred other forms of parental hysteria, the court assumes that the burden of suffering and self-sacrifice is on the parent rather than the child. All mothers and fathers don't have to put up with a Cain, but the records of the court suggest that there is no shortage of children who come close. The variety of aggravating offspring is staggering—almost as staggering as the patience and affection and fortitude with which their parents endure them.

Mr. and Mrs. Schimmel's son, Stanley, is twenty-three and has given them trouble all his life. In school he played truant and his grades were poor. He used to have terrible temper tantrums. His mother took him to the Stuyvesant Clinic for Problem Children, but after a few weeks they said there was nothing they could do for him. He quit high school and drifted from one job to another. Then he began using narcotics. His mother found a package of marijuana in his room. Later he turned to heroin. To support this habit he pawned everything he owned. He donated blood, possibly for the money but more likely, in his father's opinion, to mislead the police if he were questioned about the needle marks on his arms. He teamed up with another addict, and they broke into a friend's house while the parents were in Florida and sold all the furniture. He was arrested and put on probation for three years. He lives at home, curses his parents constantly, and sometimes strikes his mother. He stays out all night and refuses to tell them where he has been; they are afraid that he is committing more crimes. They want the court to advise them what to do about him.

These facts are given to the judges by the boy's father, a man in his fifties who never looks at his son while he is speaking.

"Do you give him money, Mr. Schimmel?" the judge asks.

"I give him money all right," says Mr. Schimmel. "Maybe he'll rob a few less houses that way."

"Is the boy's mother here with you?"

"She wouldn't come."

"She doesn't approve of your bringing these charges?"

"She approves. She knows we have to do something. But she couldn't stand it to be here."

The judges question Stanley now. He is tall, heavyset, and good-looking.

"Why don't you go out and get a steady job?" asks the businessman-judge.

"I had a lot of them. I worked as long as a year at a place. But I always had to quit."

"Why did you quit?"

"On account of my psychological problems."

"You know that you're sick and need to be taken care of?"

"Absolutely. What I'd like is a psychiatrist. My home life is very unsatisfactory. There's a lot of conflict there. Now that I'm not addicted anymore, I'm ready for intensive therapy."

"Would you go to Central Islip Hospital if we recommended that?"

"Central Islip? That's a place for drug addicts and schizos. I couldn't go to a public-type place like that. I don't think I could make any progress unless I had the full treatment that a private psychiatrist would give me. You know, one of those thirty-dollar-an-hour ones with a fancy office on Park Avenue."

"On my salary with the City License Bureau," says Mr. Schimmel, "where do I get thirty dollars an hour?"

"Your father is right," says the judge. "Your request for private therapy is a little unrealistic. Now Mrs. Richman could recommend some good people who will see you a few times at reduced fees and send you on to a clinic—"

"Sorry," says Stanley with a shrug. "I wouldn't consider any *schlock* psychiatry like that. It's Park Avenue or nothing."

In the end the judges urge Stanley's father to give him no more money and to send him out of the house.

"Fine, nothing would suit me better," Mr. Schimmel says. "And when I see in the paper one day that he was arrested for killing somebody, what do I do, change my name?"

Although the truly vicious child is rare, the good-for-nothing is fairly common. He doesn't commit crimes, take drugs, or behave violently, like Stanley Schimmel, but on the key question of going out and finding a job and no longer living off his parents, his reluctance is just as great.

Mr. and Mrs. Bosniak come to court with their son, Marcus. The judges talk to the father separately, without the other two being present.

"I have a problem with my son," he says. "He is almost twenty-seven. He went to yeshiva and now he doesn't do anything. He doesn't go out."

"Was he in the army?" asks a judge.

"He was physically unfit. I am a man who works long hours—I am a shammas in a synagogue in Patterson, New Jersey—and I don't see the boy as often as I wish. If my wife would only take more interest in his problem it would help."

"Your wife isn't close to your son?"

"She is too close to him, that's part of the trouble. She seems to be satisfied with him. She won't see anything wrong. Once, a few years ago, he worked for a while at a job, but when he came home, she said how pale and tired he looked, and this gave him a reason to quit."

"What is it you want us to do, Mr. Bosniak?"

"I want you to convince him he should learn a trade. If he agrees to learn a trade, I will help him."

"What trade? Does he know anything?"

"He doesn't know anything."

"You mentioned he went to yeshiva. What did he learn there?"

"He went to three yeshivas, but he didn't make a success. He did no homework and listened to the radio. Now we have television, he sits in the house all day and watches it. This is the first time he has been out of the house in months."

"Does your son have any friends or girls?" asks the court psychiatrist.

"He has friends that come over at night sometimes. He had a girl but he doesn't see her anymore. She got married, I think."

The businessman-judge speaks up now. "Suppose we advised you to give him no more money and to make him leave the house unless he gets a job and contributes to the rent—would you take this adivce, Mr. Bosniak?"

"*I* would take it," Bosniak says sadly. "I have even suggested it. My wife says to me, 'If you throw him out, you will have to throw me out too.'"

Bosniak is sent out of the room, and his son, Marcus, is called in. He is short and fat, and he listens and talks in a serious, cooperative manner, with many nods of agreement.

The businessman-judge begins. "Your father says you loaf around the house day and night and never go out looking for a job."

"My father told the truth," Marcus answers. "He is absolutely right. I am a great trouble to my mother and him."

"What is the reason you don't help?"

"I am very nervous. Some time ago I quit school. I was seventeen. I was idle. I had no confidence I could get a job. I didn't feel inclined to work. I was afraid I would be rejected."

"So if you were, you would go some place else," says the businessman-judge.

"You're a big boy," says the lawyer-judge. "How do you expect to make a living? How do you get money to spend and food to eat?"

"My father gives it to me. I probably would starve if he stopped giving me money."

"Your father is an elderly gentleman. How long do you think he can continue doing this?"

"Not forever. I know this. It worries me very much. I am a great trouble to—"

"Did you *ever* have a job where you brought some money?" the businessman-judge breaks in.

"I had two jobs, and each was for one day. The first job I was discharged. I was a shipping clerk. The second one was in Patterson, I worked on a lathe."

"Did you like this work?"

"No."

"You have a good racket," says the businessman-judge. "If you don't feel like working, you just don't work. I think you are making it too easy for yourself. A man of twenty-one or over usually takes care of himself —he doesn't depend on his father. I am going to suggest to your father that he stop giving you money unless you find a job."

Marcus picks this up sharply. "Did my father ask you to say that?"

"Why should he ask us?"

"It is a suggestion he has made before. I am a great trouble to my father and mother, this I know. There is no excuse for me, but it is important to understand that maybe I am not the only one to blame. Maybe there are extenuating circumstances."

"What circumstances?"

"My father has a very excitable temper. He does not know the right way to handle me. He compels me to do things that are not good for me at all. Like washing dishes late at night when I wasn't in good health. He asks me to come to the synagogue at seven in the morning so there will be enough men for the morning service. He asks me to do this even though I had to stay up late the night before, and this does not agree with me."

"You seem to be in good health," says the businessman-judge.

"I was very underweight at one time, and now I am overweight, and my father worsens this condition. His conduct and character upset me. Furthermore, he uses the heat very sparingly. This affects me badly."

"Why don't you go out?"

"The cold air affects me badly. And my father grudgingly gives me food. There is conflict about it almost daily. I can't get enough food when I want it."

"We get the impression," says the businessman-judge, "that your mother is cooperative."

"She had money from an accident, so she does me a favor and uses this for me. I don't like her to do this. I am a great trouble to her."

"You could stop being a trouble," says the businessman-judge. "You could be trained for a job. Your father is willing to send you to a trade school."

"This might be the answer to all your problems," says

the laywer-judge. "Would you be willing to go to a trade school?"

For a moment Marcus's eyes shift to the side, as if he were looking for help to come. "I think the main thing is to improve my health. The cold has affected me so that I sleep very poorly. I don't eat meat. My father doesn't give me a free choice to eat what I want."

"Your father can only give what he earns," says the businessman-judge. "Go to a trade school, and soon you'll be able to buy your own meat."

"I don't eat regular meals," says Marcus. "I get up and feel as though I were getting up in the middle of the night. I have a very poor appetite."

"Work hard at the trade school, and your appetite will improve."

Now the rabbi speaks for the first time, in a much more sympathetic voice than the other two judges have used. "You have difficulties, and you need to talk them out with someone. Have you ever thought of seeking medical help?"

"A psychiatrist, you mean? My father took me to one a long time ago. I didn't like him and I didn't like the idea of going."

"What did this doctor tell you to do?"

"He said I would be all right and I should get a job."

"Would you go to another doctor? Mrs. Richman could find someone sympathetic who could help you."

"I think a doctor would be a mistake. I think I would be wasting my time."

The businessman-judge simply can't resist this opening. "And what are you doing right now with your time? Listen to me, Marcus—you must stop taking money from your father, and you know it as well as we do. I want you to promise me that you will go out and look for a job."

The businessman-judge glares at Marcus hard, and Marcus blinks back at him for a while. Finally he give a nod. "All right, I will try."

"Good!" says the judge.

"I will try Monday."

"Why not tomorrow?" says the judge.

The judge's suggestion is put in the form of a decision —Marcus is ordered to start looking for a job first thing in the morning. And the rabbi adds to this that he is to make an appointment with a psychiatrist recommended by Mrs. Richman.

Marcus's mother has come into the room to hear this decision. She reacts strongly to the rabbi's remarks. "My son isn't out of his mind!"

"Nobody says he is, Mrs. Bosniak," the rabbi explains. "He is only in need of help. Why doesn't he work?"

"He helps his father in the synagogue. When he gets stronger, he will do more."

"Why doesn't he go out with girls? Why doesn't he visit friends?"

"He talks to people."

"Why has he stayed in the house for six months?"

"That's not true. He has gone to synagogue on Saturday a couple of times."

"Mrs. Bosniak, are you satisfied with his condition?"

"No—not satisfied. But he is not out of his mind. He just feels things, and they make him upset. That is why he had to leave the places where he worked. He is too good."

A month later Ruth Richman calls the Bosniaks to

find out how things are going. Mr. Bosniak tells her wearily that Marcus looked for a job for two days, then stopped looking, and he went to the psychiatrist only once. But Mrs. Bosniak is optimistic. "He's making improvement," she says. "He goes out of the house now."

"Where does he go?"

"He goes to the race track. I give him a few dollars . . ."

The girl or boy who hasn't married is the cause of special suffering to parents. Every year the judges see a number of distraught parents who want to know what to do about their incipient old maids and bachelors at home. Usually there isn't much the judges can say, except to tell the parents to stop worrying, stop nagging, and hope for the best. Occasionally they will encounter a situation of this sort in which the issues are much more complex and dramatic.

Berenice Kraft is thirty-two years old and unmarried when her mother, Mrs. Sadie Kraft, brings her to court. The mother and daughter live together in a house in Long Island that they own jointly, their sole inheritance from Mr. Kraft, who died ten years ago. Mrs. Kraft has worked hard hard all her life and looks it. She now is a housekeeper in a hotel.

She is obviously proud of her daughter. Before bringing out her charges, she is careful to let the judges know about all the young woman's accomplishments. She describes her daughter as a teacher, an artist, a social worker, a businesswoman, an expert stenographer, a talented maker of ceramics. Until three or four years ago, she says, her daughter didn't live in the house in Long Island but had a studio in Greenwich Village where she made her ceramics and sold them. Unfortunately the business didn't work out. Mrs. Kraft can't understand why. Her daughter's ceramics were beautiful; people just don't know what's good anymore. In short, she has never until now had anything to complain of in Berenice, except maybe that she wishes the girl would get married. There have been men, but somehow she never got married.

This brings her to her charges. A few years ago Harvey Waterman came into their lives. He is a year younger than Berenice, and he describes himself as a promoter and public relations man. He first met Berenice while she still had her studio. Later, when she had moved into the house in Long Island, Harvey Waterman suddenly appeared and proceeded to move into the house too. For the last two and a half years he has been occupying a room on the second floor, taking many of his meals with the mother and daughter, and, of course, paying nothing for rent or food. Berenice is earning no money, so Mrs. Kraft ends up supporting Waterman. She can't afford to go on like this; she isn't such a big earner herself. She keeps trying to throw him out, but Berenice keeps telling him he can stay. He is good-looking and well-educated, Mrs. Kraft admits. If he would marry Berenice and take care of her as a husband should, Mrs. Kraft would raise no objections; after all, how many prizes is her daughter going to catch at the age of thirty-two? But Waterman is a loafer, and she doesn't think he will ever propose to Berenice, and meanwhile he is spoiling her other chances. So Mrs. Kraft wants the judges to do what she hasn't been able to do herself—make Berenice send Waterman out of the house.

The judges call Berenice before them. She is tall and plain and obviously takes very little time with her clothes, her hair, or her makeup. She speaks quietly, in a genteel, "cultured" voice.

"Please tell us, Miss Kraft," the judge asks, "why you allow Mr. Waterman to live in your house without paying any rent?"

"There is a reason why Mr. Waterman hasn't paid the rent. I want to explain a terrible set of circumstances. I was outstanding and successful. I was promised a hundred dollars a week, and then it happened that this friend of mine got fired. I decided to become an artist instead of a businesswoman. I want to say that my work is very valuable. I settled in Greenwich Village and started a project. But my mother caused me to lose a lot of money—"

"You were explaining why Mr. Waterman doesn't pay the rent."

"Yes. I have papers from Albany that authorize me to start a nonprofit foundation. I thought Mr. Waterman could help me. Mr. Waterman was very good to me when I met him, and he made it possible for me to go ahead with my plans. My mother is a wonderful woman but unfortunately she dominates me. The psychiatrist told me to live alone. When I met Mr. Waterman I was heartbroken and he opened new doors to me. But Mother has always interfered in my affairs."

"About the rent?" says the judge.

"Yes, I was explaining. Mr. Waterman is also a designer, and we have mutual interests. At my mother's suggestion I asked him to stay overnight because of a terrible storm. When he returned from Mexico, he was very successful, but unfortunately the people paid him in pesos. This friend of Mr. Waterman's called me, and I sent him the money to go from Texas to New York. I sent him $85 to cover the fare. When he came up, he asked me if he could stay for a few days. Unfortunately this friend of his told my mother that he was a liar, and this created an atmosphere of suspicion in her mind."

"What does Mr. Waterman do for a living?"

"In my association with Mr. Waterman, he has created things. He is a designer and is self-employed. When he came to my house, the understanding was that he was to work together with me. Nobody shared the house with us." Suddenly, for just a moment, the genteel voice grows shrill. "I can't live all alone with my mother! I would die!"

"But I want to know about Mr. Waterman," says the rabbi. "Why does he live in your house for over two years and pay no rent?"

"I would like to explain about that," says Berenice, and her voice is quiet again. "I could have sold the house to the foundation, the inter-art foundation that I am authorized to establish, which would have given payment and be entitled to the income of the property. My mother, however, refuses to agree to this arrangement. I think it is wrong of my mother to disgrace me."

"Miss Kraft, you must consider this question," says the rabbi. "What kind of a man is Mr. Waterman that he stays in a home that is not his for over two years and he doesn't pay any rent?"

"It is because I want to provide a home for him. Twice he offered to leave but I asked him to return to me."

"Do you have a fondness for this man?"

"It is natural to have a fondness. He has given me priceless times."

"Is it a love affair?" the rabbi asks.

The question doesn't embarrass Berenice a bit. "It might have been if my mother did not interfere. His mother died and he was neglected. He was an only child, and we have a great many similarities. He won a prize for outstanding advertising. Why does my mother want him to leave the house? It would be better if *she* left the house."

The judges see that there is nothing they can say to Berenice, no way of making her listen to them. They send her out and speak to her mother. "You must realize that your daughter is sick," says the rabbi. "She should get psychiatric treatment. Mrs. Richman will arrange for her to see somebody. But you must also make an effort to get Mr. Waterman out of your house, even without your daughter's permission."

"You are half owner of the house," says the lawyer-judge. "You have the legal right to evict anybody you don't approve of. Would you like Mrs. Richman to recommend a lawyer to take care of this for you?"

Mrs. Kraft agrees to all of this. The judges decide to adjourn the case until there is more information available about Berenice's mental state. The case will be called again after the psychiatrist has examined her.

A month passes. In this time Mrs. Kraft keeps in touch with Ruth Richman and brings in a new complaint every day about Waterman and her daughter. His room is filthy and he refuses to allow her to come into it; money is missing frequently from her purse; one day he knocked Mrs. Kraft down, and she was black and blue; Berenice takes his side and claims her mother attacked him first. Ruth Richman asks her why she doesn't get in touch with the lawyer that the Board recommended and have him put Waterman out. Mrs. Kraft becomes vague at this question and soon leaves the office.

Meanwhile Mrs. Richman has arranged for Berenice to see a psychiatrist, and his report comes in. He says that Berenice is very disturbed, highly neurotic, and ought to have analytic help. As soon as she has this report, Mrs. Richman arranges for another hearing before the court.

In the week before this hearing she gets a visit from Berenice. She has come to complain about her mother. She says that the house must be sold to the foundation in order to put their life on a viable financial basis. She wants to redecorate, she wants to incorporate, she wants to rent studios and classrooms—she has all the papers for a nonprofit organization but her mother keeps spoiling these plans. She also tells Mrs. Richman, almost offhandedly, that Mr. Waterman recently asked her to marry him. Mrs. Richman asks her what her answer was. A preoccupied look comes into Berenice's eyes. "He is younger than me, you know," she says, and she changes the subject.

A few days later Mrs. Kraft is on the phone to complain that Mr. Waterman just called her a bitch. Mrs. Richman asks her if she has contacted the lawyer yet.

The next day Berenice is on the phone. She has decided that she wants to go to work. If she can find a job befitting her talents, she will be able to live independently of her mother. Somehow, though, everything depends on selling the house to the foundation. Will

Mrs. Richman kindly instruct the judges at the hearing next week to persuade her mother to permit the sale? And she would also appreciate it if Mrs. Richman could help her find the right sort of job. Perhaps with a museum or an art gallery where her knowledge of the arts will be useful.

A few days later the second hearing is held. The judges are different, but they are equipped with the transcript of a month ago and with the psychiatrist's report. They ask Berenice if she doesn't feel it might be a good idea for her to talk over her problems with a qualified doctor.

"I have been to a psychiatrist," Berenice says. "He was very helpful, but he agreed that my mother is the crux of my difficulties. At times my mother is very sweet, but it is difficult for her to understand me. Her attitude toward Mr. Waterman is entirely without understanding."

"Yes, about Mr. Waterman—"

"Mr. Waterman is someone who does public relations. He has helped me to sell works of art. He has a wide acquaintance. Since I was working with him, I gave him my bedroom and I moved into the upstairs study. We have been asked to raise money for a cause —a foundation for which I have the necessary papers. We would be very successful if my mother did not stand in the way. She listens on the telephone and tells me what to say. I have a girlfriend from my school days— and I was a very distinguished student in school—and she called me up, and my mother interrupted many times from the extension. It is her manner of scheming. I cannot blame her, she has a sickness. If it were not for her sickness, I could do something with our house. I could fix it up and make something of it. I have a talent of fixing places over. I managed real estate all my life. If my mother had helped me when I had my studio, I would be on top of the world. I have a destiny in my work. Mr. Waterman is an orphan, and so am I, except for my mother. He is alone, and we could be outstanding and successful without her opposition. She refuses to understand the value of my work."

And then, to everyone's surprise, Berenice announces that Mr. Waterman has come to the court and wishes to give his views of the situation. The judges are glad to see him. He is a tall handsome man with a big smile.

"How do you see the problem with the home?" the rabbi asks him.

"The mother interferes with the daughter," Waterman says. "There have been so many arguments with these two people, and I have to break them up. I cannot sleep at night."

"Why don't you move out?" says the businessman-judge.

"I would like to answer when Miss Kraft and Mrs. Kraft are out of the room." So the mother and daughter are asked to leave, and then Waterman says, "I would move out tomorrow if I could. But I am in a financial hole."

"The mother is in her sixties, and you are earning no money," says the rabbi. "Isn't it logical that you take the first step and leave their home?"

Waterman spreads his hands. "I have no place to go. I have to eat."

"Mrs. Kraft has the legal right to evict you," says the

lawyer-judge. "Before that happens, why don't you walk out like a gentleman?"

"I would do it if I could. I have no income. Life is a gamble."

"You should seek welfare from the city of New York, to which you're entitled."

"Save everybody a lot of unpleasantness, Mr. Waterman," says the rabbi. "Show your generous heart and move out."

"I would like to oblige you people. I am a Jewish boy. I would like to do what is right."

They work on him for a while, and in the end Waterman says, "All right, I promise to move out."

They call Berenice and Mrs. Kraft back in and tell them what Waterman has promised. Berenice cries out, "My mother has destroyed this relationship!"

The judges now render their decision. Waterman is to move out, Berenice is to continue with the psychiatrist, Mrs. Kraft is to be as understanding and forebearing as possible. End of the case.

But of course it isn't. This is one of those cases that continues for a long time after the court has officially lost interest in it. Mrs. Richman calls up Mrs. Kraft a week later and asks if Waterman has left yet. Mrs. Kraft admits that he hasn't. She says that Berenice became hysterical after the hearing and begged Waterman not to leave and finally he gave in. Mrs. Richman urges Mrs. Kraft to call the lawyer and have Waterman evicted. Mrs. Kraft says she'll think it over. After all, she would be content if Waterman would only work and pay for his food.

Five days later Mrs. Kraft calls to say that Berenice kicked her.

Two days later she calls to say that Waterman eats all day long, and her utility bills are too high.

Four days later she comes to the office and reports that Waterman's phone bill for the month is $83. Mrs. Richman talks to her a long time and finally persuades her to let the lawyer arrange for Waterman's removal from the house the next morning.

Two hours after leaving the office Mrs. Kraft calls and says she doesn't want to go through with the removal.

Two days later Berenice calls to tell Mrs. Richman that Mr. Waterman took her to Ratner's the night before and when he told the cashier he was a big public relations man he was not allowed to pay for his dinner. She also tells Mrs. Richman how much she respects and admires the Jewish Conciliation Board, how she appreciated the rabbi's kindness and concern when he questioned her in court, and how she would like to do work for his synagogue. She has had a great deal of experience handling affairs for nonprofit organizations.

Mrs. Richman asks her if she has been in touch with the psychiatrist. She says, rather surprisingly, that she has an appointment in a few days.

Two months pass. Mrs. Kraft suddenly appears in the office and says that her daughter has stopped going to the psychiatrist. For a while it seemed as if Waterman would leave the house, but he didn't. He is still there.

Mrs. Richman calls Berenice and asks her why she stopped going to the psychiatrist. Berenice answers that he was very "cruel" to her. Mrs. Richman is unable to persuade her to go back.

Then silence for a year.

Suddenly a call from Berenice. She wants to go back for psychotherapy. Why? Mr. Waterman has moved out. He has found a rich woman of fifty whom he expects to marry.

Ten minutes after Berenice's call, Mrs. Kraft comes into the office. She wants to warn Mrs. Richman that Berenice will be calling. She hopes Mrs. Richman can find another psychiatrist for Berenice. With tears in her eyes she confesses that she is sick, she fears she has cancer, she worries what will happen to Berenice if she dies. Who can help except the Board? So Mrs. Richman sets the psychiatric consultation in motion again.

That is the last she hears of the case for two years. Then she gets a letter from Berenice. Her mother has died, and Berenice blames her death on the psychiatrist. During mother's last illness Mr. Waterman got in touch with Berenice again; he said the fifty-year-old woman was a misunderstanding and he wanted to see Berenice. Mrs. Kraft got upset at this. Berenice asked the psychiatrist to reassure her mother that Mr. Waterman's return was all right, but the psychiatrist refused. "I will never forgive him for his heartlessness," Berenice writes. And she has reported him to the medical association for malpractice.

Now that her mother is gone, she writes, she has asked Mr. Waterman to move back into the house, and he has graciously accepted the offer, despite the personal sacrifice involved. They are in the process of making very exciting plans to redecorate the house so that they can sell it to the nonprofit foundation. Also she is now making ceramics with the Ten

Commandments on them, which she intends to sell to private collectors for a great deal of money. Her agent in this matter is Mr. Waterman.

Mrs. Richman calls up the medical association and tells them what she knows about Berenice Kraft. Then she washes her hands of the whole case. Berenice, it seems, will manage through the years to protect her neurosis and survive.

A problem peculiar to this community and to other immigrant communities is the child who looks down on his parents from the heights of a superior education. The cultural gap brings a great many unhappy people to court.

Mr. Rosenzweig, a small fat man in his sixties, comes to court to demand support from his wife and daughters because he is getting too old and sick to work. His daughters, both in their twenties and both unmarried, have good jobs—one is a schoolteacher, the other is a secretary—and live with his wife in an apartment on Central Park West. Rosenzweig has been separated from them for seven years.

"Where do you live now?" the judge asks.

"In Brooklyn, in a dump. With strangers."

"Why don't you live with your family?"

"I couldn't stand it. I can't live with them together. So I left."

"But why?"

"The children are too difficult for me to understand." He speaks in a thick accent, but there is no mistaking the sarcasm in his words. "They are too swell. They are too fancy for me."

The judges turn to the girls, Nettie and Harriet. They

find out each each of them earns a nice salary, but most of it goes to pay for the apartment they live in.

"Central Park West is not a cheap neighborhood," the judge says.

"Our mother isn't well," says Nettie, the younger and quieter one. "She can't work, and her health has been poor for some years. We need this apartment because she must be near the park."

"You care very much for your mother?"

"She has been like an angel to us all our lives. All the time we were growing up she worked and sacrificed for us so that we could have a good education and become cultured and improve ourselves."

"Your father didn't help?"

"Our father never did anything except sneer at us," says Harriet, the older and sharper one. "He is an ignorant man, and if he had his way we would be ignorant too."

"His world was always so cheap and vulgar," says Nettie. "He drank. He brought beer and whiskey from the saloon into our house. He drank it there with his cheap friends who couldn't even talk English."

"He made our lives bitter," says Harriet. "Only our mother saved us."

"Even so," says the judge, "a father, be he the devil himself, deserves some support from his children."

"We are willing to help him," says Nettie. "But we cannot afford to pay two rents. We want him to come and live with us. In the apartment there is an extra bed. We will take care of him there."

"As long as he behaves himself," says Harriet.

"Well, what about that Mr. Rosenzweig?" says the judge. "Your daughters have made a very generous offer. You can be reunited with your family again."

"I won't go to live with them!" Rosenzweig says. "If I wanted to be reunited, why did I bother to leave?"

"But they've made the gesture voluntarily—"

"A fine life this would be, with these fine daughters of mine! Excuse me, they're much too swell for me. What are they planning to do with me when their fancy friends come to visit? Will they shut me up in a closet, like they do with their mother, so their boyfriends won't get a look at me? All right, I like a drink once in a while. I want to have my bit of beer and make a *l'chaim*. Will my daughters let me if I'm under their roof? Thank you again, but I wouldn't do it!"

"So what do you want from them?" the judge asks.

"They should give me some money every week, I wouldn't bother them. I'll sign a paper they'll never see me again. Their fancy friends don't even have to know I'm alive."

The judges order his daughters to pay him $7.00 a week. This is the minimum amount of support they could award him, but after all he has challenged one of the deepest beliefs of the community. Education is the shining goal that every parent is supposed to want, above everything else, for his children. If the education makes the parent into dirt in his children's eyes, his duty is to accept this state of affairs meekly and keep his mouth shut.

Who is the most tormented and unfortunate parent in the records of the court? Among this multitude of sponging children, disobedient children, unmarried children, crazy children, which child is giving his parents the largest amount of suffering?

Mrs. Dora Wilenz is a widow whose younger daughter, Ruth, is neither vicious, lazy, or willful. She may, in fact, be the most well-meaning child who ever appeared before the court. Mrs. Wilenz has an older daughter who is married and lives in another city. Ruth lives with her mother. She is in her twenties, and the first thing anyone ever notices about her is how enormously fat she is.

"I want my daughter to behave herself properly, as a respectable woman should," says Mrs. Wilenz. "We are a fine family, but I am constantly ashamed of her. She has a job, she works at night. I have come to court so the judges will tell her to give up this job."

"What kind of a job?" the judge asks, but Mrs. Wilenz is now in tears.

"All my life I have had such bad luck," she sobs. "My husband died when I was a young girl with two little daughters. It wasn't easy to raise them properly, there was never a lot of money. My oldest got married to a nice boy—they should live in peace—but this one! She's already shamed me so that once I wanted to commit suicide."

She leans forward toward the judges and speaks in a lower, confidential voice. "The truth is, she isn't too bright. She doesn't know all the time what's good for her. She goes to this job every night, but she can't do this kind of work properly . . ."

All the time Mrs. Wilenz talks, her daughter Ruth stands by docile but unconcerned, as if she were listening to a story about a complete stranger. Finally the judges turn to her.

"Do you hear what your mother had to say? She's not very happy you're working at night?"

"It isn't easy to find a job these days," says Ruth in a high thin voice rather surprising from a girl of her bulk. "I looked day and night, and this was the one I found."

"How old are you?"

"I am twenty-five years old. I know you are supposed to be independent at twenty-one. It is right that I should be independent and start helping my mother."

"In this night job of yours, what kind of work do you do?"

"I am a dancer."

The judges have seen a lot, but this one catches them by surprise. They say nothing for a moment, while some of the spectators giggle.

"A what?" the judge finally asks.

"I am a tap dancer," Ruth says.

"She's not a dancer!" Mrs. Wilenz breaks in. "There's no job for her. I don't like that place where she works. I followed her once, and it is not more than a bar. I keep telling her this is no place for a decent girl, but she's so stubborn she won't listen."

"If I am not a dancer," says Ruth, "why did my boss buy me a pair of golden shoes? Yes, a pair of golden shoes, and he told me he paid $6.00 for them."

She comes out with these words eagerly, and her face looks animated for the first time. It is clear to everybody by now that the girl is mentally retarded. The spectators stop giggling.

The rabbi takes over the questioning, using his kindliest tone. "Are you working there long?"

"No, not long, Only a few weeks. Maybe five or six weeks. Or seven. Or eight."

"Do they pay you each week?"

"Till now they have paid me nothing. My boss keeps fooling me." She grins, just a bit slyly. "He thinks he's going to get away with it. So he bought me a pair of golden shoes. You should see those shoes! $6.oo he paid for them, I mean money. And he says to me that the drinks I get are also worth something. He thinks I'm a fool, but I'm not that much of a fool."

"You should give up this job," says the rabbi. "Your mother is aggravated, and it's ridiculous to work for nothing. You'd be better off to find a position in a hospital or to do housework."

The girl shakes her head. "No, I don't want to. When I was five years old my mother bought me tap-dancing shoes, and I love to dance. I have wanted to be a dancer all my life."

"Now you see the troubles I'm in?" says Mrs. Wilenz. "I don't know how to cope with her. In a few weeks I must go to the hospital for a serious operation. I don't know who to leave her with."

The rabbi addresses Ruth again. "Ruth, my dear, you must forget the dancing. This is not for you. We'll try to get a daytime job for you. So in the evening you'll be able to stay home or go out with your friends, just like all good girls do."

"I once worked with my cousin in a factory. And when I met one of the girls on the street, in a white uniform, she said she is a nurse. I worked in a hospital once long ago." Her eyes light up. "Two, three years ago. I wore a blue uniform." The light fades from her eyes. "In the factory it was ugly—I couldn't stand it— but in the hospital it was good."

"Would you like to work in a hospital again?"

Ruth frowns hard. "It would be good for me to work there. But I know they wouldn't want to take me. I am not a nurse."

"Leave that place where you are now," says the businessman-judge, "and I will see what I can do about a hospital job for you. I am on the board of one or two. But you must leave that place right away."

"No, not right away. Let me first get the money they owe me. He bought me a pair of shoes, but that is not enough. And drinks for nothing are also not enough."

"Forget the boss and the money—"

"No! This is my money! He's not going to make a fool out of me! I saw myself how he paid the other girls. The golden shoes are not for them, that's true. But he must pay me too . . ."

She starts crying like a baby. Her mother takes her in her arms to comfort her. Everybody in court looks away with embarrassment.

At last the rabbi says, "Don't cry. We will see that this man pays you. Just tell us how much he owes you—"

Ruth pulls away from her mother. "I will get my money for myself! I don't want anybody else to ask for my money! Even if I must give back the shoes. Don't think that I'm such a fool!"

The judges render no official decision. They instruct Mrs. Richman to arrange to find medical help for the girl and also to send her to the hospital to apply for a job. The mother and daughter leave together, and instantly there is an audible sigh of relief around the room.

The relief isn't likely to last long. The next case or the one after that or the one after that will bring another anguished mother and father to the court. The parade

*178*

of difficult children goes on and on, just as many today as there were fifty years ago. Parents are supposed to suffer; God has ordained it that way, as the judges and everyone else in the court know perfectly well. Most of them have children of their own.

# CHAPTER

## 12

❦ ❦
❦

# *Brothers and Sisters*

It isn't just between husbands and wives or parents and children that feelings run deep. There is almost no such thing as a casual family relationship. The ties are so close that *every* relationship is intense, a tangle of love and hate that could produce an explosion at any moment. This intensity applies particularly to brothers and sisters, who have grown up together in large families and small apartments.

The underlying assumption—that every member of a family is somehow inextricably intertwined with every other—is expressed in the old religious injunction of *halitza*. According to Mosaic law a childless widow who wishes to remarry must marry her deceased husband's brother; otherwise she must remain single. The family is presumed to have a special, almost mystical identity; in joining the family the woman has committed herself to continuing and extending this identity.

She cannot be permitted to give herself to any other family unless she has fulfilled her first commitment. Therefore, if she hasn't had a child by her late husband, she can have one by his brother, who after all partakes of the same identity, the same "blood." After biblical times the talmudic rabbis reinterpreted *halitza* and declared that the woman could be released from her obligation with the express permission of her brother-in-law; but the basic principle remained.

In the first two decades of the Jewish court the judges used to consider a number of *halitza* cases every year. The opportunities it offered for vindictiveness or downright blackmail were immense; often the brother used *halitza* to lever an extra portion of the estate out of the widow. Such cases never arise anymore; among other reasons there is a shortage of sufficiently pious widows. But the attitude *halitza* represents, and the complex feelings this attitude can arouse, is still very much part of the court's affairs.

What strikes us first is the intense bitterness and suspicion that brother-sister relationships, much like marital relationships, can generate.

Max Minkoff, a man in his sixties, complains to the judges that his sister, Fanny Eckstein, has been writing letters and making phone calls to the officers of his society, telling them that he stole the family silver from her. "All the members, the president, the vice president, they are all gossiping about me and giving me a bad name on account of her. Why does my sister say these terrible things against me?"

Mrs. Eckstein says that the whole charge is a figment of her brother's imagination; she has never been in touch with his society, never accused him of stealing any silver, never spoken two harsh words against him in her whole life.

The judges point out to Minkoff that he has no grounds for his charges. "Why don't you believe your sister, who is your flesh and blood, rather than the society, who isn't? Why do you trust a stranger and not your own sister?"

But of course the whole point is that Minkoff mistrusts his sister precisely *because* she is his sister and not a stranger; it's the intensity of his feeling for her that has turned sour and filled him with suspicion. The judges decide that he has no case against her, but he leaves the courtroom muttering curses.

What strikes us next is how often the bitterness and suspicion turn out to be well-founded. Brothers and siters can, in fact, do some truly horrible things to one another.

Beatrice Rubinoff brings her brother Max Kramer to court. She is in her forties, angry and excitable. Instead of explaining her case directly to the judges, she insists on reading out loud the letter that she wrote a month ago to Louis Richman.

"Dear Mr. Richman," the letter goes, "ten years ago my brother Max had a fruit store in which he made a poor living. He told my husband, Dave, who is a cab-driver, that there was no future in the business and he wanted to make big money. He said that my husband and my younger brother, Richie, and he could start a taxicab business as three partners. One morning a week later he came to our house and told my husband that he wouldn't get along with him and he didn't want to go into partnership with him. I now think that Max didn't like the idea of raising money and having my husband get some benefit from it. But I didn't allow any grievances because I loved my brother and knew that he loved me. We had always been a very close and affectionate family.

"Max knew that we had just had an inheritance from my husband's grandmother for $3500, and although he didn't want my husband for a partner, he sent my younger brother, Richie, to see if we would lend him this money, as more money was needed in the business. Again my husband didn't like the idea but I persuaded him to lend the money. At that time Max knew nothing about taxicabs and came to our house every morning for three weeks to get my husband to go bargain hunting for more Medallions and to take him around to consult different people. My husband worked nights and slept days, but this went on every day and kept my husband from sleeping, and we lost out on quite a bit of salary.

"In the meantime my brother Richie kept telling me to buy five Medallions with cars and go in business for myself. At that time the price of Medallions was low. I told Max I wanted to borrow money on our insurance policy and also I wanted back the money we had loaned to him—with this I would buy five Medallions. He said to me, 'Richie don't know whether he is going or coming!' and that it doesn't pay to borrow money on the policy and that it would be a hardship and a headache for him to pay back what he owes us. I trusted him fully at that time. I didn't realize the reason he wouldn't pay me back my money was because he was expanding his own business. This is why he discouraged me from getting the five Medallions. This was his way of showing gratitude for what we had done to help him.

"Three years later a man who did business with my husband wanted my husband to go into the taxicab industry with him in a big way. Again I consulted my brother Max, whom I still trusted. He scared me, saying that I might not be able to sell if I couldn't meet the payments. I felt sure he meant his advice to be for my good, so I didn't go into the business. Now I believe he was afraid that my husband might get ahead of him in the business.

"In the meantime Medallions kept rising in price. Again my brother Richie told me I had better buy while it was still possible. Again Max made the same remark that Richie knows nothing. In the meantime he himself borrowed money from the bank and bought more cabs. At that time he had about twenty cabs.

"About three years ago my husband went to a broker in the business who also has sixty or more cabs of his own. My husband asked him if he couldn't do something for him as he did not want to be a driver all the rest of his life. The broker, who knows my husband very well, asked him how much he could raise, and my husband explained that a relative would lend him most of the money. The relative was going to be my brother, and the broker agreed to put up the rest of the money for seven Medallions, and we would meet in his office the next morning to sign the papers. My husband was so excited that he called from the drugstore in the broker's office building to tell me we are made. I, in turn, phoned my lovable brother, and he promised to lend the money, and he assured us he was happy to see us get ahead, and he even offered to go with my husband to the broker's office next day to make sure the papers were all right. The minute they arrived, my brother didn't even take time to say good morning, but he gave a yell and a bang on the table, and he said, 'On what prospect are you lending him so much money?' The broker realized there was a family conflict and backed out of the deal. So it never went through.

"So it was then I realized that my brother was my worst enemy. My very dear brother, who pretended to love me so much and who was in my home more than in his own and took us out all the time. My friends and neighbors remarked that they had never known such a devoted brother. My husband used to ask me if I was married to my brother or to him. Yes, the truth is that he never wanted me to get ahead, he never wanted me to move out of my five-room dungeon, he never wanted my children to have a better education or better things in life if possible. He stabbed me in the back that has given me a life-lasting pain. As a result I am sick and emotionally and mentally upset. I have not been able to care properly for my home and my children. I spend my days crying. My husband is also sick as a result and no doctor is able to help us very much. My husband is unable to work much as a result of so much trouble and aggravation because he confided in my brother, who in turn betrayed him.

"Sincerely yours, Beatrice Rubinoff (Mrs. David Rubinoff).

PS—My brother does the repairing of our cab when necessary. I do not really appreciate this because I know that if I had my own garage I wouldn't need help from him."

When she has finished reading this letter, the judges

ask Mrs. Rubinoff their familiar, inevitable question: "What do you want us to do for you?"

"My brother has thirty-three cabs today," she answers, "and each cab at the present market price is $11,500, which gives him an income of about $200 a week. Because of his advice it has cost my husband and me over $100,000 through the years, not to mention the income we should be drawing today. I want compensation for this. I have paid a bitter price for my stupidity in trusting him, and I am entitled to compensation."

The judges ask her brother Max Kramer to reply to her charges. He is a large red-faced man, clearly used to getting what he sets out to get.

"It's true I started a cab business and had to borrow from my sister and her husband. They got it all back already with interest. The reason I never went in with my brother-in-law as a partner, he was always very lazy and didn't want to work, and the cab business is very hard work. At the time I started the business I had no idea it would be successful. I discouraged my sister from taking the risk and tried to protect her. At the time my brother-in-law wanted to enter the business the Medallions were very high, and they couldn't raise the money. I went to the broker, and he told me it wasn't wise for my brother-in-law to take over cabs at that time, which I tried to tell my sister. I never took anything away from her."

"She claims the broker was all ready to finance her husband and you ruined the deal."

"This is a lie and a dream. If a man wants to finance you, he finances you—how can a stranger talk him out of it? She has a lot of dreams. I wouldn't even have come to this court to listen to her, except . . ."

*186*

He hesitates. The rabbi-judge says, "Except what, Mr. Kramer?"

"My daughter is getting married, and I want my sister to come to the wedding."

"She tells lies about you, but you want her at your daughter's wedding?"

Kramer looks distinctly uncomfortable. "We've got a mother. She is seventy-five years of age and is very upset over this feeling between my sister and me. She is anxious to have us make up. Our mother has said that she can't go to my daughter's wedding unless my sister goes."

"You want us to persuade your sister to go to this wedding?"

"If you could do it, I would appreciate it. Frankly I'll be very happy to make peace with her. We were always so close when we were children. We lived in such harmony together. How should a business come between us?"

The judges turn to Mrs. Rubinoff. "What do you want your brother to do for you that will make everything all right? Do you want him to say 'I love you and want you to be my friend'? Do you want him to say 'I am sorry that I didn't tell you to buy taxicabs four years ago, I made a mistake'? Mr. Kramer, you'll say this to your sister, won't you?"

"All right, I'll say it." Kramer turns directly to Mrs. Rubinoff. "I'm sorry. I made a mistake."

"That is not enough," she says. "I want him to buy a few Medallions for me."

"Medallions today are $20,000 apiece!" Kramer cries.

"And I want him also," says Mrs. Rubinoff, "to admit that he lied to us and tricked us and cheated us deliberately so we wouldn't get ahead."

"Mrs. Rubinoff, this is no way to have peace," says the rabbi-judge. "Suppose you *had* purchased some cabs, and suppose Medallions had gone down instead of up, what would you now be feeling about your brother?"

"They didn't go down," she says. "He should have taken us in for a partner."

"What you are doing is a punishment to your mother," the rabbi says. "There is a happy day coming up. If you fail to go to this wedding, you are going to make your mother suffer. You must forgive him and attend the wedding for your mother's sake."

"One thing hasn't got to do with the other. I won't go."

"We will ask him to give you a token of his sympathy and his desire for peace. Mr. Kramer," the rabbi turns to him, "since you have had financial success and although your sister isn't destitute, the court suggests that you give her $1000 for a summer vacation."

"I will give it to her gladly," Kramer says.

"I will throw it back in his face," says Mrs. Rubinoff.

In the end the judges can do nothing with her, and they are forced to dismiss the case. The truth is that some of the things people do to each other—especially people who belong to the same family—are unforgiveable.

Given the bitterness of many of these disputes, the amazing thing is that they often are settled more or less happily. Conciliation does take place and sometimes in the most unlikely circumstances.

The reason for this, of course, is that the hatred between brothers and sisters usually has its roots in the love they once felt for one other; and this hatred can never quite succeed in killing their instinctive conviction that they ought to love each other again. Whether or not they are aware of it, most of the people who come before the court accept the basic assumptions implied in *halitza*. It is easier, in fact, for a married couple to stop caring about each other—because they can remember a time when they didn't even know one other, because they are conscious of having made a choice. Husbands and wives don't have to feel that they were born into their relationship, yoked together by God. It often happens, then, that warring brothers and sisters come to court not for the reasons they give but with the unconscious desire to be reconciled.

William Glogauer has been estranged from his younger brother, George, for years. Now their father has died, and William summons George to court on the charge that he refuses to contribute to the cost of the father's tombstone. George tells the judges that he is completely bewildered by this charge. Until this very moment he hasn't heard from or seen William in seven years. The letter he got from Mrs. Richman, asking him to attend the hearing, was the first indication he had that he owed money for his father's tombstone. He is perfectly willing to pay whatever his brother wants him to pay.

Then what are these two men doing in front of the judges? Why did William set up the hearing and invent the story of George's refusal to pay? And why did George come to court at all? When he received Mrs. Richman's letter, all he had to do was send a check and save himself a lot of inconvenience.

The judges understand exactly what is going on. The rabbi makes a few speeches about *sholom bais* to the two brothers, and soon there is an emotional scene complete with tears, embraces, and speeches of apology and forgiveness.

Bessie and Bertha Blitzer are sisters, both in their sixties and both unmarried. They share a three-room apartment in the Bronx. Bertha, slightly younger and a good deal more aggressive, has brought Bessie to court.

"What do you want to tell us, ladies?" the rabbi asks. "If we can be of service to you, that's what we are here for."

Bertha says, "Since she moved into the apartment about six years ago, I have been keeping it clean as much as possible. We have a refrigerator that I have been defrosting for two years. My sister does absolutely nothing. In addition she does not take care of herself. She does not keep her clothes clean and insists that everything is okay, and if I don't like it, too bad. She does not take care of her hair either. I don't mind what I do, as long as she takes care of her room and herself."

"She is not friendly," Bessie says. "When I say something, she doesn't let me. The painters told me not to move things, so I did not move them. When I am in the kitchen, she does not want me there. So I go out to eat. It annoys her because I ask questions."

"How often do you eat out?" the rabbi asks.

"A few times a week, in the evenings."

"You are sisters, and you don't eat together?"

"In the beginning we did," says Bessie, "but not now."

The rabbi consults his sheet of paper. "I see here that

your mother died ten years ago and your father fifteen years ago. If they were here now and would say to you, 'You are both my children, why don't you become more friendly and eat together?' wouldn't you do it?"

"Yes, I would," says Bessie, sniffling a little. "About my hair. I tripped and hurt my head. The heat from the hair dryer causes me pain, and I cannot go to the beauty parlor."

"She tripped because she was climbing on a chair in the closet when I told her not to," says Bertha. "Whatever I tell her she does not listen to and gets herself in a mess."

"What is your economic situation?" asks the businessman-judge.

"I am eligible for Social Security," says Bertha, "and I have some funds. I was secretary, and my firm closed down."

"I do sewing in the house," says Bessie. "I collect Social Security and have some money in trust."

"Thank you, ladies," says the rabbi-judge. "Now if you will please leave the room, we will consider our decision."

The sisters leave. The judges all agree that they must stay together if possible. Where could they go? Who would they have if not each other? But the problem is to convince them of this. The judges finally decide to try a little elementary strategy on them.

The sisters are called in again. The rabbi-judge faces them gravely. "It is very pathetic that two sisters cannot get along," he says. "Just think what your parents would feel like if they saw this. However, the way you have been living is no good. If you can't get along, it is certainly better to separate. We have decided that the two of you should live alone."

There is a long silence. The sisters just stare at the judges.

Bertha finally speaks, her voice not quite so firm as before. "I ask nothing of her except that she take better care of herself and her room. This should not be hard for her to do."

"I want to take care of my room," says Bessie. "I would do it, except she gets me so upset. She tells me to leave the kitchen."

"Sometimes I must be alone," says Bertha.

"All this merely proves to us that our decision is right," says the businessman-judge. "You are very fine people, but from what you have told us you are pretty far apart. Nothing we might say could bring you closer together. Therefore it would be best for you to go out and live separately in different homes."

Another long silence. Then Bertha says, "I have already put in an application for an apartment for myself."

Bessie turns to her, alarmed. "When did you do this?"

"Well, this is good," says the businessman-judge. "You have put in an application. Soon you will be able to move away. It is best you get settled in your new place before winter comes. It is difficult getting used to living alone during the winter."

After another pause Bertha says, "I have not actually put in the application. I asked about the application, and they said they would send it to me. I came here because I think she should try to act better."

"I will try to keep the apartment clean," says Bessie. "But she must also speak nicer to me."

"Am I to understand," says the lawyer-judge, "that you two might possibly wish to stay together in spite of your troubles?"

"I'm not convinced it would work," says the business-man-judge. "Let them separate and live alone. To be near each other and understand each other will take a great effort, which I don't think they are willing to make."

"I'll make it if she'll make it," says Bertha.

"I am not too old to make efforts," says Bessie.

The businessman and the lawyer look skeptical, but the rabbi says, "I think they could do it, gentlemen. I think we should give them the chance." He turns to the sisters. "If we decide you should stay together, will you do everything you can to work things out? You realize what the alternative is—living alone and the horrors of living alone?"

The sisters nod, and already the tears are beginning to come.

"I see you are willing to take another chance," says the rabbi. "All right, you may stay together. Keep in touch with Mrs. Richman, tell her how it's going. Thank you, girls, and good luck."

# CHAPTER

# 13

❧ ❧
❧

# *Friends and Acquaintances*

Peace is desirable outside the house too. A man's dealings with his business associates, his friends, his neighbors ought to be as harmonious as his dealings with his family. But it doesn't always work out that way. The world of this court is a jungle. Its denizens are poor and beleaguered; they have learned to be tough in order to survive. Their tendency to treat "outsiders" callously, even ruthlessly, reveals itself in many cases. One function of the court has always been to combat this tendency, to make people aware of their moral obligation to those who are not their own flesh and blood.

This function is most clearly required in disputes between people who are doing business with each other. In such disputes the judges usually try to remind the opposing parties of the human bond that unites them underneath their business differences.

A tall, stocky, ruddy-faced man in his fifties comes to court. He is wearing high rubber boots and a red woolen sweater, the costume of a fisherman. Also coming to court is a small, middle-aged lady with an air of great refinement. She seems anxious to stand as far away from this fisherman as possible.

The fisherman, whose name is Rudnick, tells his story in a loud boisterous manner, with a kind of boyish excitement. "In the marketplace where I have my fish stand," he says, "this lady, Mrs. Katz, has her grocery store. Her husband, Jacob, was my best friend. In all the world Jake Katz was the best friend I ever had. Such a man! Such honesty! The most honorable honest man I ever met—"

"So what are your charges, Mr. Rudnick?" the judge asks.

"I used to give Katz my money to hold for me when I went out fishing in the boat. And when I came back and I needed any of it, he would give it to me what I needed. One day, a few months ago, my friend went to his daughter in Buffalo, and he died there suddenly. I had about $75 with him. I waited a few weeks, then I went to this lady—my friend's wife, a fine lady—and she said she doesn't know anything about the money. He was such an honest man—I would have trusted him with anything!"

"What do you say to this, Mrs. Katz?" the judge asks.

She speaks softly, carefully keeping her eyes away from Rudnick. "I don't know what to say. What this man just told you is all news to me. My husband never mentioned a word about this man and his money. I never met this man. I never knew my husband was a friend of his. My husband introduced me to all his friends, and this man I never met."

"Couldn't your husband have kept this man's money without telling you about it?"

"It isn't possible. My husband never had to ask for loans from anybody. He had enough for me and our children. We weren't rich people, but we never lived a life of poverty."

"Excuse me," Rudnick ducks his head at Mrs. Katz respectfully, "he didn't *borrow* the money from me. I only gave it to him to *hold* for me. I had perfect confidence in him. Such a husband you had, Mrs. Katz . . ."

His compliments pour out, and impulsively he reaches out and takes her by the arm. She pulls away from him with a shudder.

"Mr. Rudnick," says the judge, "why didn't you get an IOU from Mr. Katz? Why did you give him your money at all? Why not put it in a bank?"

"You have to understand my business," Rudnick says. "I go away in the boat, I come back, I sell fish. I have a few hundred dollars at a time, never more. I need money often, but only in small amounts, a few dollars here and there. I had more confidence in Katz than a bank."

"You could write checks against a bank account."

"Yes, I could do that. Well, the truth is, checks I don't much care to write. I have to put a cross on the check—" He breaks off in embarrassment but quickly grows cheerful again and turns to Mrs. Katz. "Such a fine man he was, Mrs. Katz! For me to have a whiskey with your husband was the greatest pleasure in my life!"

"He never drank liquor," Mrs. Katz says.

"Certainly he did!" Rudnick cries. "Certainly he drank, he should rest in peace! A little whiskey occasionally, nobody enjoyed it better. He was such a friendly man. Many a night and until early morning—"

Mrs. Katz is pale now; it looks as if she might faint. The judge, seeing her agitation, interrupts Rudnick. "Mr. Rudnick, did any of the businessmen in the market ever see you give money to Mr. Katz or see him put it away for you?"

"I don't know if anyone saw. But everybody knew about it. I told everybody, why shouldn't I? Was I ashamed because I had such a fine honest friend?"

Now the judges talk over the case. Rudnick's sincerity has impressed them; nobody could disbelieve his story. Yet he has no real evidence. The only thing to do is make an appeal to Mrs. Katz's better nature. So the judges call her before them, and the rabbi makes a soft, cajoling speech asking her to recognize Rudnick's claim in the name of her late husband's honesty and friendship.

Her eyes widen with a kind of panic. "There was no friendship! My husband was never friendly with this man! He would never drink and take money from such a man! We had our friends—nice refined people—a completely different type—"

"But if the man's story is true, Mrs. Katz? He's a poor fisherman, $75 could mean a lot to him. Take pity on him—"

"Pity! He's lying! How can he say such things about my husband?"

And now the situation is clear to the judges. Mrs. Katz doesn't really care about the money. But giving it to Rudnick would be as good as admitting that a relationship did exist between him and her husband. She just can't make this admission. Refinement and gentility are ideals in her world just as much as education and charity. People may be poor, but that doesn't mean they're low class.

Sadly the judges call Rudnick in again. They tell him that they sympathize with his claim, but unfortunately he hasn't been able to produce enough evidence.

"I don't get my money back?" Rudnick looks bewildered at first, but then he shrugs and gives a good-natured grin. "All right, if you gentlemen say so. You gentlemen know about such things." He turns his grin on Mrs. Katz. "It's all right, believe me. I know that a fine lady like you, who had such a wonderful husband, wouldn't do anything—"

"I'll give him the money," says Mrs. Katz quickly. "Only he should leave me alone."

She writes out a check for $75. She doesn't give it to Rudnick, but puts it on the table in front of the judges and hurries out of the room.

Wolfgang Melniker is a well-known Yiddish writer—well-known, that is, in circles where Yiddish writers are known, unknown everywhere else. He is in his late fifties; he wears scruffy clothes, is slightly in need of a shave, but has a certain indefinable air of elegance and importance. He has come to court with charges against

Pincus Lascoff, a gloomy-looking man in his forties, just as scruffily dressed as Melniker but without the air.

"My dear people," Melniker opens his case, "it is possible you don't know who I am. I am Wolfgang Melniker, the author. Some time ago I was hired by this man, Lascoff, to edit the book that he was writing. He offered me $300 for the job, and though it is far less than my usual fee, I knew Lascoff personally—he was an admirer of my work, we had discussed literature together many times over a glass of tea at Ratner's—and so I accepted his offer. Later, after I had been engaged in the work for a while, Lascoff called me and said the book wasn't going to be published. He asked me to settle for $60, which I did—again out of friendship and respect for a fellow writer—though as yet I have received only a mere $30. A few weeks ago I learned that Lascoff's book is about to be published. Therefore I demand the rest of my $300."

Lascoff now steps forward. He is nervous, with a tendency to mumble. "Melniker did a poor editing job," Lascoff says. "All he did was change a little bit of the punctuation. I have a friend, Levy—also a first-class intellect—who looked at the manuscript and said he could do the job better, so I told him to go ahead since I was dissatisfied with Melniker."

"Why didn't you tell Mr. Melniker the truth?" asks a judge. "Why did you make up this story that your book wasn't going to be published?"

"I didn't want to insult him. You cannot tell a writer that he is not capable. So I made up a story—it was my way of saving his feelings."

"Lascoff would not have hurt me by telling me he

wasn't satisfied with my work," Melniker says. "This is the way in literary circles. God knows by now I am used to it."

"Why did you give Melniker this job in the first place?" the judge asks Lascoff.

"He is a great writer. I have admired him for some time. Until recently I have been only a businessman, in a small way, but I have felt privileged, after business hours, to sit at Melniker's feet. Naturally, when I was able to complete my own first effort at literature, I turned to Melniker for help. On account of his short stories in *The Forward,* his poetry, his dictionary on the Yiddish language, I thought he was going to do wonders for me and my book. But he did nothing. I do not think punctuation is that important."

"What about the $30 you still owe to Mr. Melniker?"

"I offered to pay it to him, but he wouldn't take it."

"He offered me this $30 yesterday," says Melniker, "after he knew we were coming before this Board. On the back of his check he wrote the words 'in full payment,' so naturally I could not accept it."

"Mr. Lascoff, have you any explanation?" says the judge. "Can you tell us why you waited so long to give Mr. Melniker his money?"

"I am having a book published," says Lascoff, looking even more miserable. "You know how much this will cost me? You know how little I will get back? Yiddish publishing—when I got into this, I had some fine ideas, all the good I was going to do—and people would know my name! I have found out a lot, believe me."

The judges talk over the case. One of them is a managing editor of *The Forward* who knows Melniker. He disqualifies himself from joining in on the decision, but the other judges insist on hearing his off-the-record opinion. So he tells them that Melniker is an expert writer and editor who must have done more than put in punctuation. He also says that he knows Levy, the man who finally did the editing job, and Levy is a hack whom Lascoff must have hired for a lot less then $300.

So the judges announce their decision: Melniker is to receive $200 in addition to the $60 already promised to him.

Lascoff objects violently. "I cannot pay! I do not have the money! The man is not entitled to it!"

"You hired him, Mr. Lascoff. You made a deal."

"Never mind I made a deal! I didn't know then—my God, you should see the bills from the printer! I am not going to beg, borrow, or steal to give him money he isn't entitled to."

"If he had done the work, would you pay?"

"Then I would have the money," says Lascoff.

"Where would you have got the money if he *had* done the job?"

"I would have gotten it. The book would have been something beautiful instead of what that no-good Levy —everything would have been different if Melniker had done what I hired him for! He is one of our greatest writers!"

"If you have such a high regard for him, Mr. Lascoff, how can you cheat him out of his money?"

This argument is too much for Lascoff, for it isn't greed or chicanery that has driven him but a dream of literary glory, a genuine belief in the ideal of literature. He pays Melniker his money and even stammers out an apology, though he is close to tears.

In friendship as well as business, in social life as well
as commercial life, peace and harmony must be maintained, and the court devotes a great deal of its time to
maintaining it. These efforts are mostly connected with
so-called society cases.

The American Jew who can afford it joins a country
club to play golf, a city club to play cards, and a beach
club to go swimming or sunbathing. The American Jew
who can't afford any of these amenities—and this includes most of the people who make use of the court—
joins a benevolent society. By and large it will satisfy his
needs quite as well as any of those more expensive
places possibly could. He never heard of golf; you can
drown at the beach; a nice game of pinochle doesn't
gain a thing from plush chairs and air-conditioning.
And the society gives him extra advantages that aren't
available to his wealthy fellow Jew with all his fancy
country clubs.

From the beginning, the earliest days of East European Jewish immigration to America, the *landsmanschaft* groups served a double purpose. They satisfied
both social and economic needs. You joined them so
that you could exchange news and play cards and drink
a glass of tea with your friends from the old country;
you also joined them so that you could get a cheap form
of insurance coverage for your family and yourself in
case of illness or death. The dues and assessments were
low—though high enough sometimes for a man with a
sweatshop job—and the benefits weren't exactly
princely, but for most of the members it was the best
they could do. Because of this double purpose the activities of a benevolent society were always fraught
with tension, suspicion, and confusion. The members

often called one another brother or sister, but you could never be quite sure whether you were dealing with the officers on a brotherly or a businesslike basis. Usually it was both at the same time.

From its inception the court has handled a great many cases dealing with the relations between societies and their members. People are constantly coming to court with complaints against their societies for high-handed tactics, rigged elections, constitutional violations, arbitrary refusal to pay benefits. In the years after the war many societies were forced to liquidate—members grew old and died off, and no young people came along to take their places—and the court was kept busy refereeing the division of assets. Today a new kind of problem has arisen: the cemetery plots that many societies bought in the old days have suddenly become valuable property. Cemetery cases are rarer than they used to be, but because of the sums involved they tend to be more complicated.

But the basic human issues remain pretty much the same. It is still possible, on nights when a great many society cases are scheduled, to watch the same scene that could have taken place fifty years ago: the courtroom full of people, a tremendous hubbub, members all over the room crying out that they've been mistreated, society officers waving their dog-eared papers and repeating, "You can't go against the constitution!" Society life is often unpleasant, sometimes downright nasty, but never less than lively. And beneath the abrasive surface are certain positive values. It just takes a while to dig down to them.

And so we must begin with the abrasive surface.

A few years after her husband's death, Mrs. Burstin takes up with a man and pretends to be his wife, though they aren't really married. For years she has belonged to a society, which now informs her that according to the bylaws anybody who remarries is no longer entitled to be a member and must sacrifice all the benefits. Poor Mrs. Burstin is torn between losing the benefits and admitting she isn't married. She chooses to confess her sin, but the officers of the society—though they know perfectly well she is telling the truth because their wives have been gossiping about her for years—claim that they don't believe her and still insist on terminating her membership.

Are they doing this out of moral indignation or delight in giving pain? The judges refuse to honor either motive and order the society to reinstate Mrs. Burstin.

Oscar Bronson is upset because when his wife died the society didn't appoint a "mourning committee" to go out to the cemetery with him. This is the society's usual procedure, and Bronson feels deeply hurt that it wasn't followed in his case. He has belonged to the society for thirty-five years and suffered much mental anguish from their lack of consideration.

The president of the society, Glatz, replies that according to the bylaws a mourning committee is to be appointed only at the discretion of the officers. If the officers don't want to form such a committee, they don't have to. In this case they didn't want to. "Bronson has often expressed himself against the officers," says Glatz. "He doesn't like how we do things, so why should we make an appearance at his wife's funeral?"

A judge says, "Do your bylaws state that a member

has to keep his mouth shut if he disagrees with your policies?"

"He has a right to talk," says Glatz, "but also we've got a right to stay away."

The judge gets furious at this. "Your personal dislike of Mr. Bronson's criticisms is no excuse for embarrassing him at his wife's funeral. Your society was very much at fault. You failed in respect to a member in good standing. We think he suffered damages in an amount that can't be compensated in money. We have decided that you shall write an apology to him, and you shall send a copy of this apology to every member of the society. You are to have mimeographed copies made at your own expense."

"Do you know what this will cost?" Glatz protests.

"We don't know, and we don't care. We think this is due to Mr. Bronson for your failing him at such a time. This is our decision. And now the rabbi will dictate to you the exact wording of your apology."

Most of the time it isn't cruelty for its own sake—the familiar sadism of small men in positions of small authority—that leads the officers of a society to oppress the members. A far more common motive is sheer unimaginative conscientiousness, the pedantry of the born bureaucrat whose passion is to make sure that the rules and regulations are strictly and literally adhered to, regardless of who gets hurt. The officerships of societies—in this community as in much larger ones—tend to be attractive to men with rigid legalistic minds.

Take the case of Aaron Mirsky, the secretary of the Novogorod Benevolent Society. Mr. Ellinbach, an older member of the society, caught a virus and had to go to the hospital. The society offers sick benefits of eight dollars a week for seven weeks, so Mr. Ellinbach has applied for his $56. Mirsky refuses to give it to him. The judges ask him why.

"First of all," Mirsky says, "can he justify why he sent his address as East Fifth Street? We have no member at that address."

"I was in the hospital and weak and dizzy from the medicines when I sent the letter to them," Ellinbach says. "So I made a mistake in the number of the street."

"This is not the point," says Mirsky. "In the constitution it requires that the letter of notification must contain the correct address."

"Is he a member of your society?" asks the judge.

"Yes," says Mirsky. "By face but not by address."

"This is a ridiculous technicality!"

"There are other reasons," says Mirsky. "Please read paragraph twelve from our constitution. It says the claimant 'must have a hospital document.'"

"You mean you would pay him his sick benefit if you had a letter from the hospital?"

"Yes, but we cannot take a man's word. We must have it in writing from the hospital."

"I gave them doctor bills and hospital receipts," says Ellinbach. "Also a note from my doctor."

"These are no good," says Mirsky. "The constitution specifically states that we must have a document from the hospital. The hospital must put it in writing, in so many words, that you were there."

"Can you get this document, Mr. Ellinbach," the judge asks.

"The hospital wants to charge me $75 extra for some electric treatments I didn't receive," Ellinbach says.

"Until this matter is straightened out, they won't give me the document. But I have all the receipts and bills—"

"We must go by our constitution," says Mirsky. "We must have a document."

"Gentlemen, we must have logic," says the judge. "It would cost this man $75 to obtain a document for you, when you agree that he's entitled to his $56. Is this justice?"

"You ought to be ashamed to go only by your constitution," says the rabbi. "This is a very reasonable claim, and you are going by technicalities that are stupid and useless."

The unanimous decision of the judges is that the society must give Ellinbach his $56.

The next day Mirsky calls up Mrs. Richman and demands a rehearing. How can the judges nullify a society's constitution? One of the judges, who was supposed to be an arbitrator, was rude and had a terribly wrong attitude toward societies in general. And the worst thing of all, the rabbi said that the constitution was stupid and useless.

Mr. Glasser has paid his society $1000 for graves for his wife, his children, and himself. He received a receipt, but the cemetery has told him that he must also have a deed to the plots. The cemetery has drawn up this deed for him, but the president of the society, Kralowitz, refuses to sign it and has persuaded the other officers not to sign it either.

"I have made up my mind that I will not sign this deed," Kralowitz tells the judges. "I have been with the society for more than thirty years, and this has never been done before. Instead of deeds our purchaser is given a marker to be put on the grave until it's going to be used."

"Suppose a member of Mr. Glasser's family dies, what then?" asks the lawyer-judge.

"Someone at the society is always available. They will tell the cemetery that it's all right to bury Mr. Glasser's relative in the grave."

"I never heard of a society that doesn't give a deed upon purchase of a plot," says the judge.

"Our synagogue sells cemetery plots to its members," says the rabbi. "We go back to 1845, and ever since then, upon full payment, the officers sign the deed and send it to the member."

"That's how you do it," says Kralowitz. "That's not how we do it."

"Your objection, as I understand it," says the judge, "is that you have never done it before. Well, I would suggest you sign the deed. You'll be signing for the society. In no way can you be held responsible as an individual."

"I can't sign for the society because we held a meeting of the officers last month and it was unanimously agreed not to give him a deed. The secretary is here right now—Mr. Fogel—and he can read to you the minutes of that meeting."

"Your meeting is irrelevant," says the judge. "A vote, even a unanimous one, cannot decide to do something illegal and unjust. Mr. Glasser has paid you his money, and he is entitled to his deed."

"During the entire term of my presidency," says Kralowitz, "nobody ever questioned my honesty!"

"Look, Mr. Kralowitz," says the rabbi, "your honesty

is not at issue. But let us assume some members of Mr. Glasser's family may pass on when you and the other officers and all of us here are no longer on this earth. It would be a difficult matter to enforce the terms of the purchase of the grave. The law of the land requires a deed, and it is the only right thing to do."

"We will have to call another meeting to decide this," Kralowitz says.

"As president of the society," says the judge, "you have to assume the responsibility. It is not incumbent on you to call another meeting."

"Morally and legally Mr. Glasser is entitled to the deed," says the rabbi. "And one more point you should consider, Mr. Kralowitz. If he doesn't get his deed, he could go to the state cemetery board or the attorney general and file a complaint against you. Isn't it the better part of prudence and wisdom to sign the deed now and not bring disgrace upon the Jewish name by dragging this matter to the civil courts?"

This argument has its effect. Kralowitz's loyalty to the community turns out to be stronger than his legalistic obstinacy. Grudgingly he signs the deed.

Before the judges can dismiss the case, a short coda is played. A little old man rises from the audience and announces in a high quavery voice that he is Mr. Fogel. "In referring to the minutes of the meeting," says Mr. Fogel, "Mr. Kralowitz referred to me as the secretary. I am not the secretary. I am the financial secretary. I wish this to be cleared up."

"Thank you, Mr. Fogel," says the judge. "We'll keep that in mind."

"Financial secretary," says Fogel as he sits down. "Not secretary."

Fortunately the legalism of society officers can be equaled and even surpassed by the legalism of some of the members. And so we are sometimes treated to the satisfying spectacle of a rigid bureaucratic secretary or president being hoisted on his petard.

Miss Pearl Slotnick's parents were members in good standing of the Vilna Benevolent Society. Her mother died on April 7, and the society paid a $100 death endowment to Miss Slotnick's father. On November 11 of the same year her father died, but the society refused to pay the $100 endowment to Miss Slotnick. "We do not owe this money," says the secretary, Mr. Kupner, "Inasmuch as there is a provision in our bylaws that states that if a mother and father die within the same year, the children are not entitled to endowments for both parents."

The clause is shown to the judges, and the argument seems to be conclusive. But Miss Slotnick turns out to be a barracks lawyer of heroic proportions. "My parents did not die in the same calendar year," she says. "Not according to the Jewish calendar. Rosh Hashonah, the New Year, came in between, therefore I'm entitled to the additional $100."

The judges agree with her and award her the money.

Old Mr. Neuhaus, one of the founding members of a society, has been expelled for not paying his dues. The officers say that they had to expel him, according to the society's constitution.

The old man approaches the judges with a serene smile and says, "They're talking about the constitution? Who made this constitution except myself?" And he proceeds to dig up an obscure clause that states that a member of twenty years standing can stop paying his dues if his annual income goes below a certain figure. Sure enough the old man is right, and the judges decide in his favor.

The pleasure that this old man takes in defeating the officers with their own weapons suggests something about the legal hairsplitting that permeates society affairs. People in this community *enjoy* this kind of hairsplitting—it is an ancient tradition, going back to the earliest disputes of the talmudic rabbis. The game of outwitting and being outwitted by your society is a lot more exciting than pinochle or golf.

Officers of societies do not prey on only the members. They also spend a lot of time fighting among themselves. The nature of being an officer seems peculiarly stimulating to the vanity of people who hold it. Every society is troubled at one time or another by intense rivalries among its big shots, and some of these rivalries explode in cases before the court.

Mr. Meyers, a former president of the society, brings it to court with a series of confused, contradictory complaints. Finally a judge says to him, "I don't see what the society has done to you. I don't see what you are complaining about." And Meyers blurts out what is really on his mind: "I don't want Ittelsohn to be president of the society! He shouldn't be a president and a manager! He has no right because he is not honorable!"

The judges are obliged to dismiss Meyer's charges, but they understand the emotions that are working in him, and so at the end of their decision they throw a sop to his vanity: "We also want to state our opinion that Mr. Meyers, in his years as president and since then, has done an excellent job with the organization."

Mrs. Bloom has been president of the society's Ladies Auxiliary for nine years. The society is now putting up a gate at its cemetery grounds, and Mrs. Bloom wants her name engraved on this gate: "Betty Bloom, President of the Ladies Auxiliary." She claims she is entitled to this honor because the president of the men's branch of the society will have *his* name and title on the gate. The officers of the society, with more than a hint of male chauvinism, refuse to honor Mrs. Bloom's request on the grounds that "the women's names are not on the stationery, so why on the gate?"

The judges at this hearing include one woman. In their deliberation on the case she says, "After all, it is not as if she is asking for the whole cemetery." And so the judges decide that Mrs. Bloom must have her name and title on the gate, but just to show that they haven't gone all the way toward Women's Liberation, they give the society permission to put Mrs. Bloom's name in smaller letters.

Old Mr. Nissenbaum has been president of his society for eighteen years. Now the members have decided to replace the presidency with a committee of ten people, to which they immediately elect Mr. Nissenbaum and his wife. But Nissenbaum is deeply offended by their action. He not only refuses to serve on the committee but he refuses to turn over the books, records, canceled checks, and bankbooks to the society.

"I am happy to give over the presidency," he says. "I am seventy years old, I'm retired, I have been president a long time, I want to enjoy life and relax. I *want* to give over the presidency, but nobody will take it. They talk to me about committees, but there is a question of legality here. I took the presidency from one man, I want to give it over to one man."

The judges realize that Nissenbaum has no legal case, but they also realize how much his pride is involved. They arrive at a formula to save his face: the members are to elect a president; Nissenbaum is to turn over the books and records to this president; then this president is to turn over his powers to the committee.

We are not told if this ingenious plan is successful. One nagging doubt—what if the new president decides, after his brief taste of power, that *he* doesn't want to give up the books and records either? As Harry Golden, who has been a judge in the court many times, put it a few years ago, "The officers in these societies are like senators—they seldom resign and they never die."

It must not be supposed from what has been reported so far that all the conflicts within the societies are the fault of misbehaving officers. The members are quite capable of making their share of trouble. Every society has its quota of obstreperous members who bring misery into the lives of conscientious officers and patient fellow members.

The most common nuisances are those who bombard the society with unreasonable demands, requests for payments or privileges that have no constitutional basis whatever.

Mr. Brickner, for example, wants his society to sell

him an extra plot in the cemetery, next to the one received for himself. On this extra plot he wants to put up benches so that his friends and relations will have a place to sit down when they come to visit him after his death. The society says that space is limited and they are very short of graves for members and their families, so they can't sell a plot for any but burial purposes. Mr. Brickner hauls them before the court and is rather miffed when the judges uphold the society.

People like Mr. Brickner are the small complainers. They want something and make a fuss to get it; as soon as they have it, they shut up again. A much greater plague to societies is the perpetual complainer, the man or woman who rises at every meeting, angrily challenges everything that anybody has done, makes endless speeches, and shouts abuse at anybody who tries to interrupt, thus effectively ruining everybody's pleasure. People like this, who seem to be in the business of making nuisances of themselves, appear frequently before the court.

Adolph Lefkowitz is in his forties. He goes in for belligerent sloppiness—frayed collar, button missing, unshined shoes. His hair is thick and bushy and flares up over his head like a sunburst.

"Mr. Lefkowitz," says the judge, "since you are the complainant, will you please start."

"Not Mr. Lefkowitz," he says. "Just Lefkowitz if you please. I don't believe in titles." Then he whirls angrily at the group of men who stand next to him and stabs his finger at them accusingly. "This is moral and legal persecution, and this is against the country!"

Once his rhetoric is stripped away, his charge

emerges. After two years of membership the society has expelled him, and he wants to know why.

"He knows why," says Berkholz, the president of the society. "We are a friendly society, and we conduct things on a democratic basis. We are very liberal in our opinions and allow all kinds, but there is a limit. Last year, for instance, we had our annual banquet on July Fourth, and when the national anthem was played, Mr. Lefkowitz refused to stand up. I didn't notice it, as I preside over the banquet, but I received some very serious complaints from other members. You understand, many of our people weren't born in this country, but they are proud of being good Americans."

"What else did he do, Mr. Berkholz?"

"A few months later we were having a drive to raise money for Israel. Mr. Lefkowitz sends out letters praising the Arabs and their cause. Of course, we have many European Jews among us who survived Hitler and lost their families, and everyone was quite annoyed. However, I felt as long as he didn't approach people personally we should try and overlook his behavior. But then a few months ago we had another banquet, raising money for the United Jewish Appeal, and he stood up just as the main speaker was being introduced and asked why we didn't give money to Arab refugees. We believe in free speech, we are a democratic organization, but certain things we have to draw the line."

"They are against civil liberties," says Lefkowitz. "They are a gestapo, only they don't know it. I ask you to make them reinstate me, in the name of American democracy."

"Mr. Lefkowitz," says the rabbi, "you are not a logical man."

"Logical! I am very logical! *They're* the ones won't listen to logic—"

"A logical man," the rabbi goes on, "accepts the consequences of his actions. You wish to be an individualist. It's difficult to be an individualist, but if you decide to be one you must understand that you will be subjected to criticism. If you champion unpopular causes, that is what happens. You must expect it and don't complain."

Lefkowitz's charges against the society are dismissed.

We could go on and on, piling up examples of the horrors and absurdities of society life. Yet, once all this has been said, it is impossible to condemn this life completely, because beneath the surface we feel that something quite different is going on. Underlying even the most horrifying and depressing society dispute is the reminder of the bond that holds these people together. The officers may be venal or callous, the membership may be full of unreasonable grabbers and complainers, but the force that has created the society in the first place is still there. A sense of fellowship, friendship, and community animates these people no matter how hard they fight or what stupid tricks they play on one another. In spite of the strong economic considerations that are inevitably a part of every society's activities, we are forced to believe in the end that the members care more about friendship than they do about money.

Menachim Greenspan, a lively little man in his sixties, complains that his society has thrown him out after forty years. The judges are used to such complaints. They know how brutal many societies can be toward their "brethren," especially those who are weak and alone. But the president and officers of this society, when they step forward, seem to be kindly, reasonable men.

"This man is deeply imbedded in my heart," says Chaiken, the president. "We know one another since the time we went to Hebrew school in the old country."

The other members of the society join in, saying how long they have known Greenspan and how much affection they have for him.

"If that is so," the judge says, "how can you turn him out of your society?"

"Believe me, it isn't what we want," Chaiken says. "For forty years he has always found some way not to pay his dues. How many times has he applied for benefits he wasn't entitled to, and we gave them to him anyway? How many times did he take out loans, and he never paid them back? Five, six times already we warned him, and every time we remembered what an old friend he is, and we didn't expel him. But there must come an end to this sometimes. We did our best for this brother, and always he did something against us, so now he is expelled."

"Even if he acted like you say," the judge says, "it's hard for him to lose all the benefits and burial rights."

"He isn't losing anything," Chaiken says. "When he was already expelled for good, I couldn't take it, my heart was heavy with anguish—let him tell it to you himself, he knows this. 'Greenspan,' I said to him, 'come, I must do something for you.' You understand, judge, this landsman of ours must have a grave, a decent funeral, and who will place a tombstone on his grave? He is, after all, our corpse. No stranger will provide a cemetery plot for him. So I went to the meeting, and I made the suggestion, and it is unanimously passed. After his death he will have a reserved grave with all the ceremonies that a dead member is entitled to have. For eternity, with the will of God, he will have everything he will need. Only during his lifetime is he expelled."

Chaiken gazes at Greenspan with great warmth and tenderness, and so do all the others.

"Is there truth in what he says, Mr. Greenspan?" the judge asks.

Greenspan can't deny it. He hangs his head and says nothing. But a little later, as the judge dismisses the case, Greenspan bursts out not angrily but with despair: "What is there to say? Eternity! The world to come they are giving me! I want to be a member again. I want to celebrate at the affairs. I want to go to the funerals. Of what use is the world to come when in this world you don't have a society?"

It is difficult not to be sad that the old societies are passing away. The members may have inflicted cruder, more brutal wounds on one another than members of country clubs and beach clubs do, but the reason was that they were closer to one another, incapable of smooth, polite, impersonal relations. This, in fact, is the secret of the court's influence over them. With all their crudeness, jealousy, and combativeness, these people felt that friendship mattered.

# CHAPTER

# 14

❦ ❦
❦

# *Worshipers*

The most religious Jews in America are probably the Hasidim, a sect that came from Europe after the war and settled in New York and a few other cities. The Hasidim seldom call upon the Jewish Conciliation Board for help. They keep to themselves and bring their problems to their own all-powerful spiritual leaders. It is among the Hasidim, in fact, that we can find the closest thing to a genuine European-style rabbinical court in America.

The people who are served by the Board make no claims to piety on a level as high as the Hasidim. Nevertheless, it would be reasonable to call them the second most religious Jews in America. This distinction is not difficult to attain; American Jews are not notably observant in religious matters. The clients of the court are much closer than most, by and large, to the old beliefs and rituals; the synagogue, the rabbi, and the sacred holidays play a much more important part in their lives. This is reflected in the large number of cases that revolve around religious or quasi-religious matters.

Disputes between synagogues and their members predominate. Some are reminiscent of business disputes or society disputes; they are characterized by the same venality or ruthlessness. But much more common in synagogue disputes is a peculiar tendency toward childishness. People who are ordinarily more or less adult in handling their affairs suddenly plunge to depths of inanity and pettiness in handling congregational affairs. Mr. Jacobson, a highly respectable merchant, donates a Torah to his synagogue, then becomes offended because in his opinion it isn't being used often enough in the services. He asks for the return of the Torah, and the rabbi tells him that this can't be done according to Jewish law. So Mr. Jacobson drives down to the synagogue to take what he considers to be his property. He talks the *shammas* into giving him the key to the room where the Torahs are kept and is just emerging from that room, his Torah under his arm, when Klingenstein, the vice president of the congregation, appears.

Now begins an epic battle out of an early Marx Brothers movie. Klingenstein yells at him, "You devil, you are awful!" Then he pulls at Jacobson's jacket, and Jacobson cries, "Take your hands off me!" and hits Klingenstein with the key. Klingenstein, bleeding from his ear, says, "I will call a special meeting of the board to discuss your conduct!" Jacobson turns and starts walking down the aisle. Klingenstein threatens to phone the police, so Jacobson says, "I am no fugitive," and sits down and waits. "But instead of phoning," Jacobson explains to the judges, "he ran up and down screaming, '*Gevalt!* A thief, a *gonif!*' Since he was not getting any police but only screaming, I got up finally, took the Torah in my car, and left."

This kind of behavior does not suggest for a moment, as cynics might like to believe, that religious people are more childish than anyone else. It is one symptom, a fairly minor one, of the ambivalent position that religion occupies in the lives of these people. On the one hand, it is fundamental, as it was in the old country; their image of themselves begins with their sense of being Jews and believing in Judaism. On the other hand, it isn't quite natural. Life in America makes them feel a little uneasy about their Jewishness; in relation to the synagogue and other appurtenances of Judaism they can't entirely keep themselves under control.

First of all, though, the belief is there. The court considers many cases every year that hinge on somebody's acceptance of Jewish rituals, customs, or superstitions. At least part of the court's job is to clear up misconceptions and settle disagreements that would never occur if faith weren't strong in the first place. (The court is not empowered, however, to deliver authoritative interpretations of the law, to set precedents of a true rabbinical court.)

Mr. Hyman J. Rabinowitz complains that his son and daughter-in-law want to name their new baby Hyman Josef. Admittedly this was the name of the daughter-in-law's late father, but it is also Mr. Rabinowitz's name, and he believes firmly in the old Jewish superstition that it is bad luck to name a child after a living relative; should this injunction be violated, the living relative will not have long to live.

The rabbi-judge assures Mr. Rabinowitz that there is nothing in the Torah, the Talmud, or any respectable Jewish commentary to justify this superstition. They even refer the matter to a talmudic authority of worldwide reputation, who gives the same assurance. But Mr. Rabinowitz refuses to accept this: "I only know what my father told me, and he was a better Jew than I am, so I can't help how I feel about it!"

The judges take his feelings seriously and order the young parents to name the child Hyman Jacob.

Mr. and Mrs. Robinson bring her father, Isaac Kornfeld, to court. The mother died ten years ago and is buried in a cemetery in Westchester. The daughter always hoped that her father would be buried there too so that she could visit his grave as well as her mother's. But Mr. Kornfeld, who is over eighty, has suddenly decided that he wants to be buried in Israel. His reason is neither perverse nor callous but deeply religious. Israel is the homeland to him, the Promised Land in which he could never live during his lifetime. It seems to him an act of piety to rest his bones there for eternity. The rabbi reminds him that his children will be hurt if he takes this step, and the old man replies, "I have thought about all this. True, the children are very very good to me, but I want to lie in Israel."

The judges can appeal to Mr. Kornfeld only on the same religious grounds that have led him to his decision. The rabbi refers to the Sabbath prayer that says that it is a great *mitzvah* to lie near your wife after death. The rabbi points out that an important religious duty for a child is to visit and do honor to his parents' grave; if Mr. Kornfeld insists on being buried in Israel, he will be depriving his daughter of the opportunity to perform this sacred duty. Furthermore, the rabbi says, "When the Messiah comes, we will all be in Israel—so you don't have to be in such a hurry."

In the end the old man is convinced, but only because he has been made to believe that being buried in America will be an even *more* pious act than being buried in Israel. "God will not be angry with you," says the rabbi as he dismisses the old man. "He knows what is in your heart and he will understand. You should live till one hundred and twenty years."

The intricacies of a religiously correct Jewish burial provide the court with several cases every year.

Mrs. Fradkin objects because the cemetery has buried an unmarried girl in the plot next to her husband. According to her strict Orthodox upbringing this is improper, undignified, in fact, scandalous. A difficult dilemma for the judges. They agree that Mrs. Fradkin is right, but they also know that Orthodox law takes a dim view of bodies being removed from their graves and buried elsewhere. In the end they order the cemetery to put up a partition between the two graves.

Old Mr. Bauer lost his leg in an operation. According to Jewish law he bought a cemetery plot and had his leg buried there, with the understanding that the rest of him would rejoin his leg in that plot when the time came. It comes ten years later, but in the interim the cemetery has changed hands, the records have been mislaid, and the old man's plot has been sold to somebody else. The Bauer children are indignant when the cemetery manager tells them that their father must be buried in a different plot. How can he be separated from his leg throughout eternity? Yet, because of the loss of records, they have no written proof that the plot really belongs to them.

The judges uphold their case, declaring that the simple presence of Mr. Bauer's leg in the grave constitutes *prima facie* evidence of his prior claim.

The religious foundations of the community are still strong, then, but even so the community has not escaped the confusion and inner conflict that have afflicted other Jewish communities in America. Here too the old faith has come up against the corrupting influence (or the reforming influence, depending on your point of view) of the modern world and American ways. This encounter, with the heartaches that often result from it, has its effect on a great many cases before the court.

It shows itself often in a certain special kind of synagogue dispute. An old man with a long holy-looking beard comes to court with a complaint against his synagogue. He himself helped to found this synagogue thirty years ago. His fellow congregants were all people who had grown up with him in the same town in Lithuania. They were all dedicated Jews, as he is, and they agreed to the condition that members of the congregation must keep the Sabbath and maintain the dietary laws. But in the last few years, because membership in the synagogue has been dwindling, the officers have decided to relax these conditions; in order to open up the synagogue to new blood, they are no longer particu-

lar about how a man keeps the holy laws. The old man,
Mr. Lenofsky, is deeply upset about this. He explains
that he has no desire to say anything against his *landsmen*; he can remember when they were children with
him in the *shtetl*, when they all went ice-skating together. He loves them as his own brothers, and he has
been through many hardships with them, but they have
taken on American ways, they neglect their religious
duties, and so their *schul* is no longer fit for him to
worship in. He has found another that will satisfy his
needs, but he is a poor man, and he can't join the new
*schul* unless the old one gives him back this year's
membership dues that he has already paid in advance.

On being questioned by the judges Mr. Lenofsky's
fellow congregants admit that things have changed and
that the old man may have legitimate reasons for feeling uncomfortable. Yet they refuse to give him back his
money. They are furious at him, yet they can't quite
explain why, even to themselves.

The judges understand. A man like Lenofsky, with
his long beard and his pious ways, is a "jewel" for any
synagogue. His presence in their midst keeps them
from confronting with absolute honesty what they
would like to ignore, that they *have* lost much of their
dedication to Judaism. If the old man leaves their synagogue, they won't be able to hide from their feelings of
guilt anymore.

But there really isn't anything the judges can do
about this. They order the synagogue to give the old
man back his money, and they urge all parties to go on
living in peace with one another.

This conflict between the old religious ways and the new becomes even more painful and virulent within the family. The heart of Judaism, after all, is in family life. And so husbands are constantly complaining to the judges that their wives won't go to the *mikveh*, the ritual baths, or that they do the housework on the Sabbath, and wives are constantly complaining that their husbands eat nonkosher food outside the house or that they play cards on Friday nights, and the complaints of parents against their impious children are legion.

Occasionally all of these feelings will come to a head in a particularly bitter and complicated family dispute.

Joel and Lillian Levin have been married for twenty-two years and have three sons. Until fourteen years ago Levin was lukewarm about religion; suddenly, at the age of thirty-seven, he became intensely Orthodox. His wife did not experience the same "conversion," and this has caused increasing conflict in the house, especially over the rearing of their sons.

Levin tells his story in a disjointed, highly emotional manner. "I have lost my two oldest sons," he begins. "They are Jewish in name only. My oldest, Morton, just got out of the army, and he doesn't even go to services on Yom Kippur. It was the same with him before the army. He asked me once to sign so that he could buy a used car. I told him no. It would break my heart if my son drove his car on the Sabbath. My second son, Eli, works in a record shop, he pretends to be a Beatle. He also has stopped having anything to do with religion. It is all the mother's fault. She keeps unreligious company. We have unreligious relatives in California, and last year she took Eli, the second boy, out to visit them.

"The third boy, Joseph, I want to save. He was bar

mitzvah last year, and I took him for that occasion to
Israel, away from his mother's influence. I wanted to
place him in an Orthodox yeshiva there, but the boy
wouldn't stay, he wanted to go home. At home it's
hopeless. He graduates from yeshiva in June, and my
wife says he will go to the public high school. This he
will do over my dead body! Once he is in the public
school he will be lost completely. Private lessons with
a good Hebrew teacher are impossible. Whenever I get
someone to study with the boy, my wife laughs and
knocks Moses. The boy still goes with me to the *schul*
on the Sabbath, but he is quickly moving away from
that too."

"Have you explained your feelings to your wife?" the
rabbi asks. "Do you discuss with her, in a reasonable
tone, the importance of a yeshiva education?"

"I discuss, but she laughs. She says that *I* never had
one. I admit this, I am sorry for it. If I had been given
a yeshiva education, I would have been more careful in
choosing a wife."

"Do you know the reason for your wife's attitude?"

"She told me something once. She said she is repay-
ing God for all the suffering she had when her family
was killed by Hitler. I told her that I also lost a family
to Hitler, but I have found my way to religion. I tell you
there is no way to do anything with her. My wife hates
everything holy. Everything that our Torah stands for
she is against. An Orthodox rabbi told me years ago you
are not premitted to live with such a woman under one
roof, it doesn't matter how many children you have."

"Why have you stayed with her then?" asks a judge.

"For the sake of the children only. Several rabbis told
me to keep fighting for their sake. But how long can a

man fight? Even a war comes to an end." Levin has trouble bringing out his next words. "So I guess there is only one thing left for me to do. Go to Israel for good. If I remain here, I'm dying off inch by inch. They are making fun of holy things, and it's killing me."

The judges turn now to Mrs. Levin.

"I think he wants too much of me," she says. Her voice is softer than her husband's, but she seems to be just as emotional. "At the time we were married, neither of us was like this, and now, after all these years, he has decided to be this way, and I don't know why. He objects to television on holidays and the Sabbath. He tells my son that God will punish him for playing ball on the Sabbath. He used to take my oldest, Morton, to *schul*, but the boy was not the type to sit still and was restless, so his father beat him up, and my son never wanted to go to *schul* after that. About this relative in California—it is his cousin, not mine. She was very good to me when I had the children, and I like her a lot and keep friendly with her. He is angry at her because her son married a *shiksa*—or rather a gentile girl, I will never say *shiksa*."

"How do you account for your husband's strong feelings?" asks the judge.

"I don't know. He served in the U.S. Army from 1941 to 1943 discharged with a 10 percent disability due to nervousness. Eight years ago he went to a psychiatrist for six months at the Veterans Administration, but then he stopped because he said he was asked too many questions and he knew what he wanted—he only wanted to be a religious Jew."

"Do you believe in a Jewish home, Mrs. Levin?" the rabbi asks.

"Yes, certainly. I have a Jewish home. I keep kosher, I light the candles on the Sabbath. But he wants too much."

"Did you ever try to dissuade your children from religion?"

"No. I always told them they could go to yeshiva."

"What about the youngest boy, Joseph?"

"He went to yeshiva for five years. Now he refuses to go back. He says he didn't learn much there. If he wanted to go back, I would let him, but I wouldn't force him."

"Can you tell us about this trip to Israel?" a judge asks.

"It was very hard for me when he took Joseph to Israel. I was very hurt, he did it without my consent. My other two sons had their bar mitzvahs here, and I also wanted the third one here, but he just picked himself up and left. I cried for two months. I didn't hear from the child for a long time, and finally I couldn't take it anymore, so I wrote to the little one, asking why he didn't write me. That is when he decided he was home-sick and wanted to come home, and not because I in any way persuaded him."

"Your husband said that you once expressed yourself that you are trying to get even with God because he killed your family by Hitler."

"I never said that. I did say only that God closed his eyes when six million Jews were killed. My husband said that they were killed because they ate unkosher and intermarried."

"Did you say that, Mr. Levin?" the rabbi asks him.

"Yes, I definitely believe that," Levin answers. "I was there and I was no youngster—I saw what was going on.

And now I see it happening to me! I sit in *schul* on Yom Kippur and see that the other children are standing near their fathers and praying—but *me*, who took my children away from *me?*" and he gives a look of hatred at his wife.

"Until your husband became religious in this way," the rabbi turns back to Mrs. Levin, "Was there ever any trouble in your married life?"

"No. We had the usual little quarrels, but it was all right."

And now the judges have a peculiar problem. What must they say to Mr. Levin? What attitude is it their duty to take? One purpose of the court is to hold the community together as a separate and distinct group, to reinforce its Jewish identity; another purpose of the court, accepted with equal conviction by the judges, is to maintain the traditional Jewish values of peace, tolerance, freedom of belief. But the question is, can these two purposes be achieved at the same time, or do they rigidly exclude each other?

In the Levin case the court seems to decide for freedom. The rabbi lectures Levin sternly: "I think that the God who makes us hate other people is not the Jewish God. The atmosphere in your home is too religious. Tolerance should be taken into consideration." And when Levin declares, "I am an Orthodox Jew! You ask me to be tolerant of what is wrong!" the rabbi almost loses his temper. "I don't think you really know what it means to be an Orthodox Jew, Mr. Levin! Religion must come from the heart. It is not something that can be forced on someone." Nevertheless, with all this emphasis on "tolerance," the judges also make it clear that in their view Levin's family *ought* to be just as devout and observant as he wants them to be. "*You* returned to Judaism after thirty-seven years," says the rabbi, "so why can't you believe your sons will one day return?" And one of the judges says, "It is no true love to love a child only when he is good, because then there is no cost to that love. The true love comes when the child is behaving badly."

Levin is an extreme case, perhaps a pathological one, yet he does raise a perplexing issue: Doesn't the atmosphere of tolerance in America encourage the backsliding from the faith that all devout Jews deplore in their children? And the judges, while displaying how humane and civilized they are, have actually evaded any direct confrontation of this issue. But, of course, they *can't* confront the issue directly. They are neither theologians nor lawmakers but arbitrators attempting to deal on a day-to-day basis with the world as they find it. If this world is confused and ambivalent, the judges are forced by the nature of their job to reflect the confusion and ambivalence in their decisions.

Nowhere is the court's (and the community's) ambivalence more clearly revealed than in its attitude toward the outside world, "them." It would be pointless for even the most dedicated Jew to deny that American Jewry comes to a good deal of its sense of identity and its religious behavior as a reaction against the gentiles. We have seen already that one of the chief purposes of the court is to protect the dignity of the Jewish name. Protect it from what and for whom? Obviously this purpose makes no sense at all unless it is seen as a deep concern for the opinion of the gentiles.

This concern, of course, is firmly based in history.

Long experience has taught Jews first of all to care what
non-Jews think of them and secondly to expect the
worst. In the community served by the court—a community somewhat more cut off from American society
than most American Jewish communities are—dealings
with non-Jews are usually colored by suspicion, hostility, and fear. The judges, to the extent that they are
*from* this community, share these feelings; to the extent that they have transcended this community, they
try to temper and even dissipate these feelings, to become a kind of bridge between their clients and the
outside world.

An angry son who is being asked to increase his support of his old mother charges that his sister, who lives
with the old lady, once allowed her to be taken to a
Christian hospital, "and there the *goyim* tried to poison
her!" This charge makes a very bad impression on the
judges. One of them says, "What would you think if a
Christian complained in a court that his mother was
almost poisoned in a Jewish hospital? We must trust
each other and know we are all brothers!" Similarly, a
young wife discovers after a year of marriage that her
husband was brought up by Italian foster parents after
his real mother walked out on him and that he visits
their graves in a Catholic cemetery regularly. This up-
sets her terribly; she is convinced that she has married
a traitor to his religion. But the judges tell her that her
husband's foster parents were good people who loved
him as tenderly as any Jewish parents could, and so she
must be grateful to them and feel glad that he respects
their memory.

On the other hand, the judges display a much harsher
attitude in dealing with the Samuels case. Mr. Samuels's

little grandson, Alvin, was born a Jew. A few months later the boy's mother, Mr. Samuels's daughter, died. The son-in-law married a Catholic girl, and the little boy is now being brought up as a Catholic. Mr. Samuels has decided to make a will, and he feels that his grandson Alvin—though he and Mrs. Samuels refuse to visit their former son-in-law—ought to be included in his will on an equal basis with his other four grandchildren: "His mother is dead, and after all she was my daughter." Mrs. Samuels doesn't want the boy included in her husband's will at all; the boy is a Catholic and therefore no longer alive for her. The judges are asked to settle this disagreement.

After much deliberation they give a modified assent to Mrs. Samuels's opinion. The child has a right to a "token share" of his grandfather's estate, but certainly not to an equal share with the "legitimate" grandchildren.

As might be expected, the court's and the community's attitude toward the gentile world coalesces most dramatically around that most sensitive and controversial issue, intermarriage. "My daughter married a gentile," says a distraught mother. "Twenty-three years old, and she's failed in life!"

Intermarriage has been increasing among young Jews in America. This is true even in the community served by the court; every year the court's records show a larger number of cases involving intermarriage. In dealing with these cases, the judges are sometimes hard put to retain their objectivity and impartial manner, for this problem is not without its personal connotations for them; several of the judges, in lecturing a litigant about his child's intermarriage, mention that one of their own children has intermarried too. Nevertheless, they make every effort to uphold, even in this emotion-charged area, traditional Jewish values of fairness, reason, and humaneness.

In one respect, in fact, the community differs from the judges, at least from the concensus among the judges. In the community the feeling against intermarriage is so strong that no circumstance can mitigate it —not even the gentile mate's conversion to Judaism. Once a gentile, always a gentile. This notion, which is directly contrary to Jewish law, is so deeply imbedded in the community's consciousness that no amount of talmudic scholarship can blast it out. The feeling goes way beyond logic. Mrs. Oster, for instance, has a daughter who married a gentile; he then converted to Judaism. After explaining to the court how long and hard she worked to persuade Mr. Oster to accept his new son-in-law, Mrs. Oster finishes up, "I forgive my daughter but I cannot forget. This injury I will always harbor, always have pain about. It doesn't matter how I accept, I really can't"

This is one of those questions in which the judges try to serve as leaders of the community, not merely as reflectors. They see themselves as standing for law against prejudice, for generosity against blind hostility. In many cases we can see them struggling to make the community as enlightened as they are.

Mr. and Mrs. Weinberg come to court in hopes that the judges can settle their disagreement about their son, Nathan. Both these people, though they are only in their early fifties, look old and tired; their eyes are red, as if they haven't had much sleep lately.

"The problem is with my son and wife," says Mr. Weinberg. "He is twenty-nine years old and has all the fine qualities one can wish for. He is a professor at a university and is a graduate of Princeton college. He kept kosher through his school years and observed the Sabbath. Whenever he met a girl whom he liked, he asked her about keeping a kosher home. He was disappointed in them, as they showed no interest in a kosher home. He eventually met a non-Jewish girl at the university, they fell in love with each other, and she has been preparing for conversion to Judaism under the tutelage of the Hillel rabbi at the university. About a month ago he told us about his plan to marry this girl."

All the time he talks, his wife is weeping softly by his side. He stops and gives a look at her, half sadly and half impatiently. Then he hurries on, "It is heartbreaking for us to accept this. I had my rabbi, a close friend of ours, go out there to meet the girl. He assured us that she seems to be very sincere about her conversion and promises to observe the Jewish laws and keep everything necessary for a Jewish Orthodox woman to observe. This girl is giving up a quarter-of-a-million-dollar inheritance from her grandfather in order to marry our son. Her grandfather left this money to her under the condition that she doesn't marry a Negro or a Jew. The couple will not be married until one and a half years after her conversion, which is requested by the rabbi. My wife does not want to listen to the rabbi, who told us to accept this as a final decision of our son. She wants to give our son up and wants me to give him up too.

How can you make up your mind that your child is not yours?"

The rabbi-judge says, "You feel you could reconcile yourself to this situation, Mr. Weinberg?"

"I don't like it, but I could reconcile myself. We are people of means, we are now retired, though young, and we could enjoy life. As it is, I am ashamed to look at people. I stopped accepting honors at my synagogue since I heard of this terrible fact, and I don't know what to do with myself. Not a soul knows about it. It would be terrible if our friends knew."

He takes out a letter and shows it to the judges. It is a letter from his friend the rabbi, trying to reassure Mr. and Mrs. Weinberg that the girl's conversion will be a true one and that they need not be so despondent.

The judges now turn to Mrs. Weinberg. "Please tell us what your feelings are."

She is barely able to stop sobbing. "My husband told the whole story. I have nothing to add. I don't want to know my son any longer, and this is all I have to say."

Mr. Weinberg puts in, "She does not allow me to sign her name on the letters I write to our son."

The rabbi asks, "Mrs. Weinberg, are your reasons religious ones?"

"Yes."

"These things happened in ancient times and are happening now," says the rabbi. "Judaism has a way of dealing with them."

"My son always said it could never happen to him. He promised me on many occasions, because since he went out of town we had such discussions a number of times. I told him now to make a choice between his girl and

me, and he apparently has made his choice. I will have
nothing to do with him as long as I live."

"But as we understand it," says the rabbi, "this girl is
willing to accept the Jewish religion in the fullest sense
of the word. Have you seen this letter from your own
rabbi and your friend? She is now being prepared for
conversion in the Orthodox manner, and your son
promises you that he will have a true Jewish home."

"This girl has three brothers and a mother," says Mrs.
Weinberg. "Is it likely she will break all relations with
them? You cannot stop her from seeing her family after
she is married."

"But why must she stop seeing her family?" says the
lawyer-judge. "I too have a daughter-in-law who was a
gentile converted. She sees her family often, but she
keeps a better Jewish home than my wife and me."

"Is your main concern that your son isn't strong
enough to keep his wife religious?" the rabbi asks. "If
you could be sure that he will succeed in having her
adhere to all Orthodox laws, would you feel differently
about her?"

Mrs. Weinberg shakes her head. "No. I have already
made up my mind."

"Would you be more inclined to accept a Jewish girl
who *refuses* to observe the Jewish laws?"

Mrs. Weinberg hesitates just a moment, then nods
firmly. "If she is Jewish, yes. I would rather have one
that is not observant than a non-Jewess."

The rabbi assumes a grave manner and uses his impressive rabbinical voice. "The Jewish law, Mrs. Weinberg, says that once she converts to Judaism she is Jewish. Have you never read the story of Ruth in the Bible?

A Jew is permitted to marry a converted woman as long as she takes upon herself all the duties of an Orthodox Jewish wife. Now that you know what is written in the Bible, don't you think you should reconsider your decision?"

"You must be careful," says the court psychiatrist, "not to overdo your attitude. You don't want your son to become disillusioned in you and turn away from his feelings of Orthodoxy—"

"Which he certainly possesses," adds the rabbi, "for he is preparing to live a true Jewish life once he marries this girl!"

This bombardment simply makes Mrs. Weinberg raise her voice. "Never, never! If he could do this to me, I will never want him again. My husband can accept him if he wants to, but I will leave my husband and I don't want to see or know any of my family or friends if such a thing could happen to me."

"This is what she keeps telling me," says Mr. Weinberg. "She will leave me and everybody and run away to forget everyone she has ever known. What should I do? On top of all my misfortunes my wife is going to leave me."

The rabbi and the other judges keep telling Mrs. Weinberg what they have told her already and finally put it in the form of a decision. As long as her son's wife has agreed to embrace the Jewish faith, to abide by all the duties required of a Jewish wife, and to bring up her children in accordance with the laws of Judaism, Mrs. Weinberg is ordered not to reject her son.

"I will never change my mind," says Mrs. Weinberg loudly and clearly. Then she marches out of the room, with her husband hurrying after her.

Abner Gersh has belonged to a benevolent society for forty-three years. He arranged for his first three sons, when they got married, to become members of his society. His fourth son has just married a gentile girl who converted to Judaism, was sanctioned by an Orthodox rabbi, and observes all the proper rituals and laws. Mr. Gersh now wants this son and his wife to join the society too, but the officers have refused to accept them for membership. In fact, Mr. Hirschberg, the secretary, asked Mr. Gersh to leave the society himself. Mr. Gersh explains to the judges that the humiliation is crushing him. When he walks the street, he feels that his neighbors are pointing at him and saying that his son married a *shiksa*; he cannot make people believe the truth because the society is making a liar out of him. He wants the court to correct this great injustice by ordering the society to take in his son and daughter-in-law.

The judges first question the president of the society, Mr. Snyder, a large man with a self-assured manner.

"According to Jewish law," says the rabbi, "this woman is a Jewess, and she must be accepted as such. Therefore, if Mr. Gersh wants his son and daughter-in-law to become members, why shouldn't they be accepted?"

"We choose our members," says Snyder. "We don't want *them*."

"This man has belonged to your society for over forty years," says a judge, "and he has several children. Did you ever meet son number one, son number two, or son number three? What do you have against son number four?"

"Our constitution," says Snyder, "clearly states that no member should belong to the society who doesn't live up to the highest moral and ethical standards."

"And how does this man fall short?" asks the rabbi. "Does he hit his wife? Does he steal? According to Jewish law hasn't he married a Jewish woman?"

"Then take him into *your* society," says Snyder.

The secretary, Hirschberg, is called up. He is smaller than Snyder and more unctuous.

The judge says to him, "Do you think it is right to hurt a man who belonged to your organization for forty-three years and was a good member?"

"When you mention that I hurt my brother," says Hirschberg, "I would not say yes or no. I am asking only one question. If this woman is like an American Jewish woman, this is no good. She must be like a good European Jewish woman, she should go to the *mikveh* and so on. Otherwise I—"

"Does your daughter go to the *mikveh*?" the rabbi breaks in.

"I don't know, and I wouldn't ask her."

"Then what right do you have to judge this woman? Do you have the right to question the sanction of the rabbi?"

Hirschberg and Snyder try to protest, but the judges won't let them get out anything more. "It is our decision right here and now that your organization must accept this gentleman's son and daughter-in-law as full members of the society, and the case is closed."

At moments like these we find ourselves loving the judges. There are other moments when we find ourselves feeling rather sorry for them.

In the case of Mr. Gersh's daughter-in-law the moral issue is clear, and the judges can take a firm stand, at ease with their consciences even though they may be at odds with community prejudices. But how are they to deal with their consciences in the case that follows?

Mrs. Ehrenkrantz is a widow whose son, Benjamin, is a sergeant in the army and plans to make this his career. When she first comes to Louis Richman, she tells him that her son has just married a Korean woman who is twenty years older than he and has three grown daughters. In front of the judges she begins her testimony by saying, "Last year I lost my husband, and then I am informed that my son married an Indian."

Later in her testimony she says, "I must have money from my son so that I can pay the doctor bills for my daughter, who is ill due to this son who married a black woman."

The truth seems to be that her son married a girl of Syrian descent, a year or two older than he, with an infant son. But the worst of it is that the new daughter-in-law is a Catholic and that Benjamin has converted to Catholicism.

The judges keep telling Mrs. Ehrenkrantz that the marriage and the conversion are *faits accomplis* and that she had better be sensible and realistic and accept them. Yet it is clear from their questioning of Benjamin Ehrenkrantz that their own ability to accept the inevitable is under a severe strain.

"Who performed the ceremony?" asks a judge.

"A Catholic priest," says Benjamin.

"Did you become a convert?"

"Yes."

"Was she married before?"

"Yes, she was. She has a child."

"As a Catholic, how could she marry again?" the rabbi-judge puts in eagerly. "Perhaps it is not recognized—"

"Her first husband died," Benjamin says.

"Do you go to church on Sunday?" asks another judge.

"Yes."

"Did you realize the effect your marriage would have on your mother."

"I realized she would take it out on my father, who was living at the time, and on my sister."

"It is a regrettable thing that this happened," says the judge. "It might have been better had you married a Jewish girl. But you didn't, and so we feel that your mother must face the facts. She must stop thinking of you as her enemy, and then maybe you will be willing to give her the money she asks for—"

"Suppose you renounced your Catholicism," says the rabbi thoughtfully, "would your wife go on living with you?"

"I will not do that," Benjamin says.

"You *believe* in the Catholic religion?" asks the rabbi.

"It doesn't mean too much to me one way or another. But it is important to my wife."

"Since you don't believe in Catholicism," says another judge, "why don't you renounce it and appease your mother?"

"Because I prefer to appease my wife."

"Why not appease them both?" says the rabbi. "Just as you attend church, why not also attend synagogue? If you can make your mother feel that you are still Jewish at heart—"

"I don't know if I am."

"Of course you are," says a judge. "We are all Jewish at heart. Now let us discuss this matter of the money—"

They go into a detailed financial discussion, with the sergeant explaining just how much his income and expenses come to.

In the middle of this the rabbi suddenly says, "Do you think your wife would give up Catholicism?"

"No," Benjamin says.

"You could explain to her the values of Judaism—"

"I believe I live a good life. That is the important thing, whether you are Jewish or Christian."

"Christianity is an offshoot of the Jewish religion," says one of the judges. "You ought to get some books from the library and read up on Judaism. It will do you good and make you appreciate your heritage."

"I have read the Old Testament," Benjamin says.

"I will give you some other books," says the rabbi, "and possibly your wife can read them too."

After much more negotiation the decision on Benjamin's financial responsibility to his mother is made. Mrs. Ehrenkrantz gets what she wants, but she starts crying anyway.

"Don't cry, don't cry," says the rabbi. "According to Jewish law he has not become a Catholic. To us he is still Jewish."

We may smile at the earnest efforts of this set of judges to "face facts" and to keep the peace at all costs. But surely there is also something admirable, even noble, about their patience. At any rate, not every judge is capable of so much restraint. In one case the emotional pressure was so intense that it brought about a rare occurrence—a public disagreement between two of the judges.

Mrs. Solomon tells the court that her son, Burton, has just married a gentile girl and converted to Christianity. She wants to know what she should do. The businessman-judge speaks to her gently; he advises her not to withdraw her love from the boy, not to alienate him by anger, but rather to be tactful and forebearing and to suffer in silence, for who can be sure that he won't want to return to the fold someday?

In the middle of the judge's speech the rabbi interrupts sharply: "As far as Jewish law is concerned, Mrs. Solomon, all relationship between you and your son is cut off! You have lost a son!"

"We can't turn back the past," says the conciliatory judge. "What can this mother do but keep in touch with the boy and let him know that she is always ready—"

"I don't think this case belongs to us," says the rabbi. "There is no conciliation possible here. The relationship between him and his parents is finished—that is the law."

"I don't think we can enforce the rigidity of the law. We must see if we can reunite this family. Mrs. Solomon, you can only help him with the love in your heart. You must accept him no matter what he did."

"You have given him life, and this is how he shows his gratitude," says the rabbi. "All you can do is reject him!"

Most people in the community would probably agree with the rabbi.

# CHAPTER

# 15

❦ ❦
❦

# *Old People*

And so, after a hectic life of courting, marrying, bringing up children, going to family parties, making a little money, playing cards with friends, and worshiping God, the citizen of our community wakes up one morning and finds that he has grown old. Do the records of the court suggest that his old age shows any unique characteristics? Are his—or her—declining years any different from anybody else's?

Parents are supposed to take care of their children until those children grow up. In return, when parents grow old and weak, their children are supposed to take care of *them.* One judge put it succinctly in a recent case: "All of you children are responsible for the upkeep of your father. It is your duty and not the duty of the city or the state to take care of him. You ought to be ashamed to argue about this."

Just as parents are obligated to a child despite his moral shortcomings, the child is required to overlook these shortcomings in his parents. Mr. Abraham walked out on his wife and children twenty-five years ago. His wife remarried, and now the children are grown and helping to support their mother and stepfather, though they aren't too rich themselves. Suddenly their father reappears. Abraham is nearly seventy, sick and destitute. He demands, with all the old arrogance that his children remember so well, that they contribute to his support.

"They are willing to give money to this stepfather, this stranger," Abraham says. "But me, their flesh and blood, they spit upon."

Despite the obvious awfulness of the old man, the judges decide that his children must each pay him six dollars a week. An old father, even though he is a scoundrel, cannot be thrown out on the street without a piece of bread.

An old lady, Mrs. Ascher, is small, wrinkled, neatly but poorly dressed. She stands before the judges and listens, bewildered and confused, while her grown children, grouped around her, argue angrily among themselves and with the judges about how much money each of them should contribute to her support.

One daughter has a sick husband and needs all her money for medicines. Another daughter's husband just went bankrupt. A third daughter already contributes ten dollars a week but complains that "it is breaking my back." She wants her contribution reduced. Everything seems to depend on the two sons.

The judge questions the oldest son, Leon.

*Old People*

"How much do you earn, Mr. Ascher?"
"I have two children and earn about two hundred dollars a week."
"I am a lawyer. Do you know if this got into court they would hang you?"
"Why?"
"Because you are making that money and not supporting your mother properly."
"My youngest brother has sixty to a hundred men working for him. He spends seven thousand dollars a year on entertainment. If I give, he should give a lot more."
"All this is irrelevant," says the rabbi. "We are not interested in what you think about how much your brother earns. You are responsible for yourself, not for him."
"You mentioned," says a judge, "that your wife also works and earns one hundred dollars a week. Couldn't you use some of that money toward the support of your mother?"
"No. My wife uses that money for her pleasures. I say again—I will give twenty dollars a month but not more."
"It is truly a shame," says the rabbi. "I would like to speak to you in ten years, after you have had all kinds of trouble from *your* sons."
The younger brother, Seymour, appears before the judges.
"How much will you give?"
"Not a cent. I can't pay."
"Your brother says you have plenty of money."
"Let him find it, he can have it."

"You could stop smoking and give the money for your mother."

"I don't smoke anyway."

"Your brother has offered twenty dollars a month. Can't you pay at least that much toward your mother's upkeep?"

"I can't give one dollar."

"We are putting this in the record," says the judge. "May God be with you."

The decision is that each child must pay twenty dollars a month to the mother. There are loud protests at this from every one of them, while the mother stands by, watches, and trembles.

Old Mr. Baron's son explains why he won't give money to his father.

"What does he need it for? There are things he can do without."

"What things are you talking about?" asks the judge.

"I'm referring to a particular habit that he has and can do without."

"How would you know what your father can do without?"

"I'm referring to the fact that he drinks."

"Well, that is not so bad," says the rabbi. "Your father is a lonesome old man, and he has to have something to keep him happy."

"When you say a thing like that," the judge says to the son, "you are crushing the dignity that your father has."

And the son is ordered to pay support.

# Old People

Mr. Cohen, a shabby old man, comes angrily to court. Ranged against him are the board of directors of a convalescent home for old people. The members of the board are much younger than Mr. Cohen. They are well-dressed and elegant-looking and mostly women.

Mr. Cohen explains that when this institution was started twenty-six years ago by a rabbi and his wife, Mr. Cohen devoted his time and efforts and money to the place. "I raised money from my friends. I gave them tea, sugar, chickens. I blew the shofar in their synagogue and prayed for them, and all this I did for nothing, as a mitzvah. More than twenty years I did this. And the rabbi promised me that someday, when I was old and couldn't work anymore, I would have in this home a room, the best room in the place, and I would be taken care of till the end. Over twenty years I worked, and the rabbi made this promise."

"So what are your charges?" the judge asks.

"Today this home has become a swell place. Only people with money come there. The rabbi is gone, the rebbitzen is gone—suddenly there are presidents and directors and boards. And I'm not even allowed to come in there and see what's going on. And to give me a room to live in, even a not so good room, they don't even want to hear about it! For twenty years this place is like my flesh and blood—I brought in chickens, I blew the shofar, and the rabbi promised me—"

The committee from the home put their spokeswoman forward. Her name is Mrs. Deutsch, and she speaks in educated tones.

"Our institution has a system," she says. "It has rules and regulations. We pride ourselves on being well administered. It takes a great deal of money to keep up

249

an institution like ours. We don't remain open for getting a few pounds of tea or blowing a shofar. We simply can't take that sort of thing into account."

"Don't you admit," the judge asks, "that this man put in his work in the past?"

"Of course we admit that. He did a great deal for the institution in its early days, and everybody is grateful to him. But he can't seem to understand that things have changed. He's used to being a boss. He comes in at all hours and yells at the staff and makes trouble. As if he owned the place."

"Maybe if you gave him a room—"

"We can't do that. Our home isn't the way it used to be. It's only for sick people now, the elderly sick. There are no rooms for healthy people like him. We recognize our debt to this old gentleman, and we've made him the best offer we can. We've offered to find a room for him at some other institution, one that serves elderly people who *aren't* sick. We'll put him there at our expense—"

"I won't go to any institution," says the old man. "This is my home. I brought in the tea, the sugar—I couldn't count how many chickens! I blew the shofar, and the rabbi promised me!"

"But the rabbi isn't here any more," the judge says. "This home is a different place now. It's a new environment—"

"To me it's the same place. In my heart it doesn't change."

The judges work out the best compromise they can. The board of directors is to find a room for Mr. Cohen to live in, at their expense, and he is to come to the home to take all his meals.

# Old People

This doesn't satisfy the old man. He can't understand what the world is coming to when even a Jewish court refuses to honor the promise of a rabbi.

Mr. Fink wants his money back from the old-age home that his father used to live in. He had to withdraw his father because conditions there were impossible. "Various inmates informed us he was being pushed around by other inmates. He couldn't hear well, was tripped on occasion, hit in the face, his glasses were broken. His false teeth had to be repaired and shoes had to be bought for him. Also we were informed that he struck someone, but the person he struck had antagonized him. One day when I came to see him someone was pulling his hat."

The director of the home speaks in its defense. "Mr. Fink doesn't understand that there is nothing to be done about such things. Inmates are going to argue and fight among one another. When people get older, they are like children."

The judges dismiss Mr. Fink's case.

Mrs. Goldmuntz admits that she has been urging her husband to cut down on his support of his old father. She justifies herself by referring to the old man's "extravagance." He is supposed to be destitute, yet he pawned his last ring to buy himself an expensive new suit.

Old Mr. Goldmuntz confesses that this is true. "I am a person who likes everything to be just right," he says. "I needed a suit, and it had to be just right."

"Why didn't you ask your son to buy you a suit?" says the judge.

251

The old man shakes his head. "I am sorry, I cannot get used to people giving me things. I worked all my life for my money. I enjoyed giving presents to my children and my grandchildren. Now I feel fallen. Like a nobody. Instead of being a person who gives, I am a person who begs. I am no more the person I was."

The judges decide that Mr. Goldmuntz is entitled to his suit and support.

Mr. Greenwald is thin, small, with a yellow wrinkled face and a bare head too large for his shrunken body. He looks almost like a wax dummy. In a quavery voice he says, "I am a man in my seventies. I was in business for myself, as most fine people are. Ten years ago my wife died, and since then everything has changed for me. Everything seems to have left me, like a dream. Today I have only illnesses. I have had all sorts of illnesses. Whatever illness you can think of, I've had it."

"You have children, don't you?" the judge asks.

"Children! Once there were three of them. They are living somewhere today. I have no children, and I don't need any children."

"They why have you come to court?"

"I have come to court to tell you about myself. I have got myself into a real ugly old age. My worst enemy I wouldn't wish it on. Old people usually have a little joy in the last years, but I have got bitter agonizing last years."

"What do you want us to do about this?"

"There is nothing that can be done about it. I have come to court only to tell you. Now I will leave and make an end to my life even today."

## Old People

The judges refer him to a psychiatrist who specializes in geriatric cases.

Mr. Hausman, a middle-aged bachelor living in a small apartment with his mother, brings charges against an old couple, Mr. and Mrs. Ide, who live in the apartment above his. He claims they make noise all night. "My mother can't close her eyes on account of them!"

"What do they do," asks the judge, "make parties, dance all night? They are over eighty years old."

"They move their beds. They go all over the floor. They make my head spin. My mother says something must be done."

The Ides are frail and wispy; moving from their seats to the judges' bench, they hardly make a sound. They both look scared.

"This man persecutes us," Mr. Ide says. "What noise can we make? It happens sometimes you have to get out of bed at night. So we get up, and we are afraid to move, we walk on tiptoes."

"Tell them about the stick," says Mrs. Ide.

"This man below us," says Mr. Ide, "he keeps a stick near his bed. The least little step we take, he starts clopping with that stick on the ceiling. He even made a hole in the ceiling."

"Tell them about the landlord," says Mrs. Ide.

"The landlord said he will bring this man to court to repair the ceiling," says Mr. Ide. "Gentlemen, why doesn't he leave us alone, he and his mother? I ask them, I beg them—please, people, let us have peace in our old age!"

The judges suggest that the two families should exchange apartments.

Mrs. Jaglom, who is seventy-three, complains that her husband, who is seventy-seven, keeps pestering her every day to have sexual relations with him. But for Mrs. Jaglom this is no longer possible.

"I am a sick woman with two hundred sixty blood pressure," she says, "and I am dizzy, and every day he would come to me. He keeps talking love. Does a man of seventy-seven have to torture a woman every day? He is a murderer."

The judge lectures Mr. Jaglom kindly but firmly. "Our opinion is that your needs are not right. This woman is the weaker person and she should be catered to. At this age it is too much to expect from her. Our sympathy is with her and not with you. Mr. Jaglom you ought to become interested in social functions."

"I am interested in social functions," says Mr. Jaglom, with a grin. "She is the one who isn't interested."

Mr. and Mrs. Kahn are both in their seventies. He looks tired and forlorn, she looks bright-eyed and energetic; there is even something a bit flirtatious in her manner.

Mrs. Kahn's complaint is that a few months ago her husband left her and paid money to put himself in an old-age home. He said to her, "Let the children look after you." Then he turned over what remained in his bank account to her, and off he went. She wants him to come out of the old-age home and start living with her again.

"How many years are you married?" asks the judge.

"We are married fifty-five years," says Mr. Kahn.

"Fifty-three years," says Mrs. Kahn.

"How old are you both?" asks the judge.

"I am seventy-nine years old," Mr. Kahn begins.

"He doesn't know what he's talking about," Mrs. Kahn interrupts. "He's seventy-seven years."

Mr. Kahn gives a sigh. "I am seventy-nine, and she is seventy-five."

"No, I am sixty-nine years old, which I just celebrated," says Mrs. Kahn.

"She tries to push old age away," says Mr. Kahn. "This is the trouble between us."

"He makes himself older than he is," she says. "Because he retired from work, he acts like his life is a dead end. He should leave that place, with only old men around him. He should live with me. Between us, on our Social Security, we will have a good time."

"A good time!" Mr. Kahn gives a groan. "In the home I have found my place. I want this to be my last home. I want to be alone and quiet. With her I never had enough quiet. She never treated me right. She never even sewed a button into my clothes. Now I am an old man, I want only peace and quiet."

"I want love!" says Mrs. Kahn. "And also I've got a few complaints too. My golden ring he took—ten years ago—and he never returned it to me. I want him to explain what he did with it. And also the woman he went to in Columbus, Ohio, when he was a salesman. All this I want him to explain. He goes into an old-age home so he won't have to explain."

"Enough, enough," says Mr. Kahn, holding his hands to his ears.

The judges understand the situation clearly. Old age has caught up to him but not to her. He wants to die away peacefully; she wants all the pleasure and excitement of their marriage, including the scenes and the accusations.

The judges explain to her, as patiently as possible, that nobody can force her husband to leave the old-age home and live with her if he doesn't want to.

This ends the hearing. But Mr. Kahn and his wife encounter each other in the hall outside the courtroom. She goes up to him angrily, "You ought to be ashamed of yourself, acting this way—an old man like you!"

"So let me be one," he says. "Why do you make such a fuss? You are also in your seventies."

"If I *am* seventy-five, so what?" she cries. "You took away my golden ring! You are a hold-up man!"

"And what about my citizenship papers?" he answers, a gleam beginning to appear in his eyes. "I asked you for them when I went into the home. How come you never gave them to me?"

"You don't get any papers until—"

"They belong to me! You don't have the right—"
He stops himself, looks a bit confused. Then the gleam fades, and he gives his weary sigh. "Enough, enough," he says. He hurries away from her, down the hall.

She stares after him, then she turns to another old lady, her friend, who came to court with her. "Oh God," says Mrs. Kahn. "What kind of life do I have?"

# Old People

Old Mrs. Kaufman has only one living relative, her nephew, Ernest Leeds. For a long time he has been visiting her and supporting her. Suddenly she develops a terrible fear that he is trying to hurt her.

"He is a bad person, not a good character," she tells the judges. "He asked me to sign a paper, he even brought a notary public with him. He did not explain to me what I sign. He never sent to me a copy."

"What do you want now?" the judge asks.

"He should return the signed paper to me. He is my sister's son—that is all we have left of our family from Germany. Let him return this signed paper to me, that's all—that is what I want from him. I took care of him from childhood up."

The judges call the nephew, Mr. Leeds, who is a high school teacher and a very respectable-looking man. He explains that the paper his aunt signed was a request to the German government for reparations on jewelry and silver that was taken from her family by the Nazis. He couldn't give her a copy of the request because she signed only one copy. He has tried to explain to her many times what she signed, but she always cuts him off and says she doesn't believe him. She even showed up at his principal's office once and accused him of forging her signature in order to cheat her.

"There was a terrible scene," Leeds says. "She yelled and screamed, and I couldn't get her out of there. It was very embarrassing. And the craziest part was, that night she called me up at home and said to me, as if nothing had happened, 'Ernie, you sounded this morning like you've got a cold. I hope you're wrapping up warm and drinking a lot of fruit juice.' When I got the letter from Mrs. Richman that my aunt was bringing me up on charges, I decided to come—because maybe she will listen to reason from you gentlemen."

The judges explain carefully to Mrs. Kaufman that her fears are unfounded, that her nephew can do her no harm with her signature, and that she will soon be getting some extra money. "Sleep soundly, don't worry," the rabbi says to her. But the old lady goes away looking worried.

A very old man, Mr. Peck, appears with a complaint against his neighbor. The old man gets out the first sentence or two of his story, then suddenly grows so upset and excited and red in the face that everyone in the court is afraid he will drop dead on the spot. He takes a pill, then proceeds to call his neighbor names. The judges try to calm him down and get him back to his story, but Mr. Peck gets angrier and more incoherent. He pulls papers from his pocket and waves them in the air; nobody can understand what these papers are supposed to be. Then he starts flinging abuse at the judges and ends up calling them "Goyim!" He storms out of the room.

Half an hour later, while the judges are hearing another case, Mr. Peck storms into the room again, shakes his fist and calls the judges "goyim!" again, and storms out. His case never does get heard.

Mr. Maurice Propper, a little man in his seventies with an ingratiating grin, appears before the court. Before coming to his charges, he introduces himself: "I am not just an ordinary person. I go to concerts. I read books. I have read the works of Leon Uris and other modern novelists."

The judges persuade him finally to explain what he is doing in court.

"I am not married," he says. "I am for many years a boarder in people's houses. I have lived with many different people, but I never had an experience like that I just had."

"What has happened?" the judge asks.

"I have lived with these people"—he points to the defendants, a middle-aged couple named Raschbaum —"for over eight months. And now they have taken away from me my basin, and they won't give it back to me."

"Excuse me," says the judge, "your what?"

"My basin. They took it away from me."

"Because of a basin you had to come to court?"

"But do you know what kind of basin it was?" The old man gets more excited, his eyes shining. "You've never seen anything like it in your life! You can't even get it for money. Since I got this basin, I've been taking care of it as though it was a precious jewel. And all of a sudden it got lost, they took it away."

"I still don't understand what kind of basin this could be that you had to come here to court," says the judge. "And what did you need it for?"

"I knew you would not understand," says Propper forlornly. "I had many years ago paid $25 for it. It's like a crystal—in the center it's like a mirror. Such clear cut glass. I washed myself, and when I looked into it, it was like a mirror, that's how it was clear and beautiful. Each little dot you can see because of the clearness."

Mr. and Mrs. Raschbaum swear that they don't know what he is talking about. "I never saw this kind of a cut-glass dish," says Mrs. Raschbaum. "He's angry because we asked him to find another room. For a while we felt sorry for him, but finally we had to ask him to leave. He's a crazy old bachelor!"

"And now he comes to you with this story of a basin," says Mr. Raschbaum. "Who would ever dream of taking away any of his things?"

"Let them not start with their lies!" Propper says. "I insist they give me back my basin! So clear I could see in it my face—"

The judges cut off his speech in praise of his basin. They tell him he has no proof of his charges and dismiss the case.

Propper turns red and starts screaming. "I want my basin! I will not stop at anything!"

Mrs. Rosenthal, in her seventies, claims that her niece owes her ten dollars. At first she presents her case quite calmly and persuasively. But then she says, "You must get me this ten dollars, or I am a slave to my niece."

This puzzles the judges. They question Mrs. Rosenthal further, and at last the whole story comes out. "With this ten dollars my niece bought herself a radio. Now she talks to me from that radio. Wherever I may be, she talks to me from the radio, and no matter what she says I can't talk back to her. If I don't get back my ten dollars, I will go crazy." Suddenly she stops, her face twists up in agony, then she cries out, "It's happening now! I can hear my niece now! She's cursing me on the radio!"

## Old People

"But your niece is standing right here," says the judge. "Look at her. She isn't talking on any radio."
"Why don't you help me?" Mrs. Rosenthal pleads. "You help so many people, why can't you help me?"
The judges recommend psychiatric care. They explain it to the old lady very discreetly so that they won't frighten her. "Listen to what Mrs. Richman tells you. She knows what to do. She will take you to the right doctor, and he will fix you up, and the radio will stop talking, you will be all right."

Old Mrs. Schneiderman, sobbing, brings her husband to court.
"We are married fifty-three years or more," she says, "and my husband is a very good man, I thought, but it happened that he talked. Perhaps it would have been better if he hadn't, but he did."
"Talked about what?" the judge asks.
"About the past. Suddenly one day he began to tell me stories. Then he would deny them. Then he would tell them to me again."
"But what kind of stories?"
"He told me one time and another time, the story was never the same. Once he would say, 'I went with a woman from the neighborhood.' Then he would say, 'I went with a woman from the office where I used to work.' I have wonderful children—my husband and I worked hard—we shoveled coal when we were young —" She breaks down crying.
"What would you like from us?" the rabbi asks her.
"I want you to tell me," Mrs. Schneiderman says, "can a man love his wife when he is with someone else?"

She breaks down again. So the judges turn to her husband.

"Mr. Schneiderman, is it true?"

"It is true. It happened once or twice, but I stopped, and I never did it again."

"How long ago did it happen?"

"About four or five years ago."

The judges look at the old man. He is eighty at least and so frail that he can hardly keep steady on his feet. "Four or five years ago, Mr. Schneiderman, you had an affair with a woman?"

"That is right."

"Who was she? Where did you meet her?"

"I met her—she was someone I met."

"How old was she?"

"She was younger than me. Very young. Also beautiful."

The judges look at him awhile longer, then turn back to Mrs. Schneiderman. "Do you still love your husband?" asks the rabbi.

"I don't know. We are together in the house. I was twenty-three when we met, and he was twenty-four. He was never a bad man, and he never spoke rough. Yes, I still love him."

"You are a very fine couple," says the rabbi, "and you have had a good life together for fifty-three years. Whatever may have happened—sometimes, when we get older, we imagine things. But if it did happen, he should be forgiven, that is why there is Yom Kippur. Go on loving each other and have much happiness for one hundred and twenty years. All the judges concur in this decision."

## Old People

All in all, then, old people in this community don't seem to be much different from old people in any other community. A few variations in dress and dialect, nothing deeper than that. Old age is the same calamity everywhere.

# CHAPTER

# 16

*Hopes*

The court may be growing old too. Things have changed a lot in America since 1920. The court has made its efforts to keep up with the times—it embraces modern theories about mental illness, it has become knowledgeable about the pitfalls of the welfare state—but somehow we get the feeling that it, and the community it represents, haven't changed as much as the rest of the world. The actual number of cases in the court has shown no sharp decrease in the last few decades, but the average age of the litigants does seem to be getting older. And I suspect that the average age of the judges is older too.

It used to be rare to see people under twenty-five in the court. It is now rare to see people under forty. If young people do appear, it is usually under protest or out of respect for their parents. A condescending sort of respect, I'm afraid. "We thought we should humor the old folks, so here we are." In a recent case, when the judge told an eighteen-year-old girl that "a rabbi, a businessman, and a lawyer have come to this decision, so you must abide by it," she could hardly keep herself from giggling. What was that awesome triumverate supposed to mean to her? In her world you couldn't find a better way to discredit a course of action than to stamp it with the approval of rabbis, businessmen, and lawyers.

I am not suggesting that the court is now ready for the burial society. It still has a lot of life ahead of it. It will last as long as the community it serves, and that community, unless something very unexpected occurs, has a few more generations to go. But the years of the court from now on will be its declining years. It has entered its old age—a much more dignified and useful old age, I feel sure, than what many of its clients endure.

Being old, however, does not necessarily make it obsolete. It can still perform an important function in bringing relief, consolation, and practical assistance to those who will turn to it. And it can go further than that. It can teach us something, if we are willing to learn. Out of its half century of success it has three lessons to give us—all of them applicable to the world beyond the court's "jurisdiction," all of them embodied in nearly every case described in this book.

First, justice, under certain circumstances, can be done more effectively by the community than by the state. In America we tend to believe—and our whole system of trials, penalties, appeals, and so on is based on this belief—that the law must be a machine. Justice must be not only blind but deaf, dumb, unthinking, and bloodless—in short, dead. Out of this belief we have created a juggernaut that rolls along ruthlessly and mindlessly, chewing up whatever comes into its path, grinding it to a pulp of uniform pretested quality, and spitting it out in the form of verdicts and sentences.

There *is* something to be said for this method of dispensing justice. It certainly reduces (though it does not eliminate entirely) the possibilities of corruption, favoritism, and coercion. Machines are seldom influenced by class or race prejudices; they are much harder to bribe or intimidate than human beings. With all its faults, a system based on clear-cut objective rules of evidence and procedure probably leads to fewer miscarriages of justice in criminal cases.

But criminal cases form a minority of the cases that come to our courts. Disputes between man and the state are much less common than disputes between men and other men. And in such disputes true justice may be as much involved with the personalities of the disputants, their peculiar standards of morality, their economic and social conditions, their half-conscious motives and half-expressed desires, the lives they will have to go back to after they leave the court, as it is with the specific issues of the case. Ready-to-wear justice is almost certain to be ill-fitting when it is draped over the conflict between a husband and a wife, a landlord and a tenant, a social club and a member, a boss and his employee, a couple of friends who have fallen out. Tailor-made justice seems to be required.

But tailor-made justice, like tailor-made suits, will be practical only if the tailor can devote a lot of time and personal attention to the customer. The judge's decision will be worthless unless he knows, in much more than a cursory way, the man he is judging. And not only the man but the world he comes from, the values his society lives by, the nuances of the words he uses. Such knowledge is possible only in a community court, where the judge and the judged have a mutual trust and an understanding based on a kind of family feeling. The decentralization of justice has other, more obviously practical advantages, notably the chance it offers to speed up trials while reducing their back-breaking costs. But its chief advantage, admittedly not easy to measure, is that it can transform the judicial process from a juggernaut into an occupation for civilized human beings.

The second lesson we might learn from the court is that men can settle their differences reasonably and fairly without banishing pity, tolerance, joy, and even humor from their deliberations. Emotion and common sense are not necessarily incompatible; inflexible logic is not the only means or even the best means for bringing peace and order into human affairs.

Some people observing the activites of the court are offended by what they consider to be its inconsistency, its indulgence in "sloppy thinking." The charge is absolutely correct. The judges of the court may have small minds—in this respect they are pretty much like most of us—but at least consistency is not one of their hobgoblins. They recognize instinctively that they are dealing with one of the most malleable, volatile, unpredictable, "inconsistent" materials ever created, human nature. The mixture of toughness and compassion, pragmatism and idealism with which they approach their duties seems to me completely appropriate. The proof is how often it works. People are more willing to believe what you tell them, to make the attempt to grow and change, if they feel you have been talking to them as people, not as abstractions.

And the third lesson we can learn from the court is —be skeptical. Whatever the system of law, however wise and kind the judges, however closely knit the community, human beings are going to fail much of the time when they try to solve the problems of other human beings. It is all very well to recommend *sholom bais* to a warring husband and wife; the chances are that the war will flare up again as soon as the couple gets home. It is all very well to tell the son who pleads poverty that he must support his old father; but how can you be sure that you shouldn't have believed his plea, that your disbelief wasn't caused by your dislike of his personality or the color of his tie? Fallibility is the common denominator of all cultures, all systems, all theories, all the works of man. You had better resign yourself to this if you are going into the business of setting up a court.

And within the limits of your resignation, of course, you are entitled to a modicum of optimism. Maybe, as the war between that husband and wife is about to get hot, one of them will stop and remember what the judges said and refrain just this once from bringing out the unforgiveable insult. Maybe those two business partners who have been at each other's throats for years will find in the compromise that the judges suggested to them just the excuse they need to be friends again. After all, it's happened before.

It's happened so often, in fact, that other groups in our society might well take the Jewish court as a model for further experiments in community justice. Blacks, chicanos, ethnic minorities, all those who feel intimidated, misunderstood, and betrayed by the "outside" courts should seriously consider setting up "conciliation boards," with alterations, of course, to reflect their own values and mores. At least this idea offers hope—within the limits of human fallibility. And the juggernaut offers nothing at all.

# Postlude

We cannot leave the court until we settle the dispute between Max Warshaw and the Yehupetz Benevolent Society. These people have been standing by for a long time, waiting for a decision in their case.

Warshaw's late father, as you probably remember, signed a document in which he gave up all his benefits in return for being released from his obligation of paying dues of ten dollars per year. The old man died two years later, at the age of eighty-five, and his son Max is trying to collect the $300 death endowment. The judges are shocked at the society's underhanded tactics, but nobody can deny that old Warshaw's signature is genuine or that he was in his right mind when he signed.

What will the judges' decision in this case be?

By this time we ought to know them well enough to make a good guess. After lecturing the society angrily about its callousness and unscrupulousness, the judges order it to pay Warshaw the sum of $150, half the death endowment.

It may be objected that this decision makes no sense at all from a logical point of view. If the judges believe that documents that have been clearly understood and voluntarily signed must be binding, then the society should not be made to pay anything. If they believe that humane and moral considerations are more important than documents, then the society should be made to pay the full endowment of $300. Which principle are they trying to affirm?

The truth is, they believe in both principles, and they are trying to affirm them both at once. And this, of course, is exactly what we would expect them to do.

# *Note*

## On the Research in This Book

At every session of the Jewish Conciliation Board, a
stenographer takes down all the testimony, then types
it up and puts the transcript in the Board's files. These
files are complete from 1952 to the present day. There
used to be complete files from 1920 to 1951, but a few
years ago they were all lost in storage. A sad accident
for the researcher, though the Executive Director and
her colleagues are much too busy with the Board's cur-
rent activities to worry about its past.

There are two ways in which some of the pre-1952
cases can be reconstructed. In 1932 Rabbi Samuel Buckler, a co-founder of the Board, wrote a book called *Cohen Comes First*, in which he summarized thirty or
forty cases from the first twelve years of the court's life.
The historical value of this work is immense — there is
simply no other source for this material — but the dramatic value is negligible. Rabbi Buckler reduces the

cases to their bare essentials and deals primarily with the points of talmudic law that they raise. His book, despite its Milt Gross style title, is really designed for specialists. I have made use of it in the sections discussing the early history of the court, but I have not taken any specific cases from it.

The second source of information about the pre-1952 court is *The Jewish Daily Forward,* New York's leading Yiddish-language newspaper. Since the mid-1930's *The Forward* has been publishing human interest articles about the court's cases. These articles are priceless to the researcher, but they are also rather frustrating. *The Forward* never recounts *all* of the court's cases, only those that its reporter thinks will be of interest to his special readership; the articles are written in Yiddish, with the judges and litigants speaking Yiddish, even though the actual proceedings may have been in English; and *The Forward* hardly ever assigns a date to the cases, probably because it uses this feature as filler that can be thrown into the paper whenever hard news is scarce.

Also the quality of *The Forward's* reporting is highly variable. Until the late 1940's court cases were written up by a journalist of the old school who signed himself Leadpencil. His articles tended to be short on facts and dialogue but long on purple prose and philosophical speculation. They are fun to read, and they have certainly helped to give me a sense of the community, but I have been unable to use more than three or four of the cases he describes.

Leadpencil was succeeded by Issac Metzker, who still reports the court for *The Forward* today. His work is a big improvement—clear, detailed, with a sharp ear for

speech and a sharp eye for significant touches. It does
seem sometimes that Metzker's cases are less colorful
and dramatic than Leadpencil's were, but this may be
attributable less to Metzker's taste than to Leadpencil's
baroque imagination. Nevertheless, I have used only a
few of the cases reported by Metzker because the years
he covers are by and large the same years covered by
the Board's extant files.

And so the great majority of cases described in this
book have been taken from the Board's files between
1952 and 1971. Whenever possible I have repeated the
case verbatim, only interpolating "he said" and "she
said" from time to time. It hasn't always been possible,
however. Some of the transcripts are detailed and complete; others are skimpy or disorganized or obscure.
Everything seems to depend on the individual stenographer. I have been obliged, therefore, to edit cases in
a number of ways.

First of all, I have cut much of the long-winded and
pointless repetition that human beings, when they
have stories to tell, are prone to indulge in. Second, I
have cut irrelevancies and sidetracks, unless they seem
to cast light on the main issues of a case or unless they
are amusing or interesting in themselves. Third, the
transcripts are sometimes badly organized, as if the
stenographer had jotted down everything that was said
but, in her haste, had typed it up in no particular order.
I have tried to make sense out of such cases by rearrang-
ing the elements in what seems the logical order. Admittedly this means that I have exercised personal judgment and departed from strict "objective truth," but to
have left these cases in a state of chaos would have been
to serve no truth at all. Fourth, in some of the tran-

scripts there are strange gaps. For instance, a question is asked, the answer is not given, yet three speeches later somebody refers to this answer. Obviously the stenographer has nodded. I have approached this difficulty very cautiously, but sometimes I have felt it necessary, rather than sacrifice the whole case, to use my common sense to reconstruct the missing piece of dialogue.

These changes have been forced on me by the condition of the Board's files and by my determination to re-create the life of the court as vividly as possible. I do not feel that I have been led to any important or unreasonable distortions. I have, however, made two other types of distortion deliberately, in a good cause. It is essential that none of the people whose cases are described here should suffer any embarrassment. Therefore I have invented all the names and have made them quite different from the real names. And whenever a specific fact seemed likely, however slightly, to give away the litigant's identity, I have changed that fact. If I say that a baker from Brooklyn is suing his aunt for $78, the truth may be that a butcher from the Bronx is suing his uncle for $115.